*"Because of the oppression of the weak and
the groaning of the needy, I will now arise,"
says the LORD. "I will protect them from
those who malign them." And the words of
the Lord are flawless, like silver refined in
a furnace of clay, purified seven times.*
Psalm 12:5-6

*'Untouchability' is far worse than slavery,
for the latter may be abolished by statute.
It will take more than a law to remove this
stigma from the people of India.
Nothing less than the aroused opinion of
the world can do it.*
Dr B.R. Ambedkar 30th Nov 1930

IN THE FURNACE OF CLAY

A STORY OF FAITH, FAILURE AND GRACE THAT LED TO A
COMMITMENT TO FIGHT FOR DALIT FREEDOM.

SIMON HAWTHORNE

Life
Association

In the Furnace of Clay
By Simon Hawthorne
Copyright 2011 by Simon Hawthorne
Second Edition 2013

ISBN 978-0-9568905-0-4

Published by
Life Association Ltd
Sitch House,
Taxal,
Whaley Bridge,
High Peak,
SK23 7EA
England

Tel: +44 1663 734374
Email: info@lifeassociation.org.uk
Web: www.lifeassociation.org.uk

Cover design by Stephen T.C. Morris
Typesetting by Elaine Sharples www.typesetter.org.uk
Printed and bound in India

With special thanks to;

Julia who has suffered too many bad of my bad ideas over the years, along with a few good ones, yet has stuck with me through our most testing times. The best is yet to come.

Paul and Gill Nadin for their prayer and financial support at our most needy time and without whom this charity would not have flourished as it has.

Paul Morley for introducing me to mission in the Developing World and for his friendship and shared sense of adventure over many years.

To Stephen Morris who fortunately has no interest in money so has given his substantial design talent to Life Association and Dalit Candles for little more than board and lodging.

To my brother Mike, for the painful job of correcting my numerous, grammatical errors.

To Paul and Lynn Bowden who arrived one day as angels do and fortunately decided to stay.

To our amazing and growing band of supporters without whom our work would not be possible.

IN THE FURNACE OF CLAY

CONTENTS

FOREWORD

In December 2007 the various businesses that I had set up and managed for 30 years failed and I was forced to make my staff redundant and close the doors on a lifetime's work. Several years earlier my wife Julia and I had put our house up as security for the business and offered additional personal guarantees, believing that two new businesses we had started merited such commitment. When the Northern Rock requested assistance from the Bank of England it triggered a shock wave through the economy and left us as a casualty with heavy borrowings. We lost our family home of 20 years and were wiped out financially.

I have been encouraged to write this book by John Kirkby, the founder of Christians Against Poverty. Quite simply the parallels in our lives are remarkable and having printed many thousands of copies of his own book and testimony, I am interested in seeing if this book and my story will also raise awareness for the Dalit people of India. Both John and I suffered spectacular failure before going into full time ministry and believe as a result of our difficulties, gained a greater heart for the poor. I hope that my own story will be an encouragement of God's amazing grace through testing times. In addition, many people have asked for more information about the work of Life Association amongst the Dalits, and I hope this book will provide that.

I have also recorded my early years as a – well, a juvenile delinquent to be honest, and as a testimony of God's amazing grace and his ability to recycle all the rubbish in our lives and make good from it. I hope it will be an encouragement to parents who similarly struggle with their own adolescent children. I tell, as honestly as I can, the awfulness and sense of hopelessness that overcame me when my business failed – and as I sought to make sense of my faith in it all. I wish to encourage other business people who inevitably find that business may sometimes be cruel. Above all I hope it raises awareness of our Dalit brothers and sisters in India and gives them a voice.

CHAPTER 1

MY EARLY YEARS

Every story has a beginning and my story begins in Cheadle, Cheshire where I grew up in a Christian home, with parents wholly committed to sending their children to church or Sunday school for as long as their offspring were compliant. In my case it was until I was 11 years of age, at which time I made their lives so miserable with my complaints that they eventually gave up. I know their intentions were good, but the mind numbing awfulness of my introduction to Christianity, with its drearily delivered Psalms and liturgy, has left me with a lifetime of resistance to formalised religion. This is hardly surprising when you consider how little the Anglican 1662 prayer book relates to someone of that age. It would be a long time before I would voluntarily walk through the doors of an Anglican church again and amazing that I ever came to fall in love with the Anglican Communion.

Due to the uncompromising system of the 11 plus, I was educated at Moseley Hall Grammar School, whilst my colleagues who struggled with exam's – or had just had a bad day – but I am sure were no less intelligent, were dispatched, along with the stigma attached, to Broadway secondary modern.

I remain convinced that Moseley Hall modelled itself on an educational establishment from a Dickens novel, complete with Beadle and numerous methods of corporal punishment. Most of the staff wore mortar boards and cloaks and bore more resemblance to museum curators, than a modern educational establishment. This eccentric nature of the school may have been partly attributable to the Headmaster, an elderly and poor sighted gentleman who we only ever referred to as – The Beak. He had been recruited in 1951 and was still in place in the late seventies. I recall one occasion when a sixth former had grown his hair to waist length when the Beak spotted him and ordered him to have it cut, and report to his office in the morning. He duly obliged with his hair tucked neatly down the back of his blazer, and the Beak, whose failing eyesight meant he was unable to see more than several yards in front of himself, complemented the student on his greatly improved appearance.

The Hawthorne brothers at
2 Hambleton Rd, Heald Green.
Michael at the back, Simon with the
badge and Andy on the tricycle.

Other memorable eccentrics on the staff were Abbey, a superbly descriptive nick name for someone who resembled an ancient and crumbling monument. The French teacher, Growler, was so named for obvious reasons and another antediluvian gentleman, suitably named, Weary Wilson, taught Geography. I am unsure who had named the Physics teacher – Cluck – though it always seemed oddly appropriate.

It was common knowledge that several staff members enjoyed watching young boys being thrashed, apparently because the Deputy Head required a witness to be present. A certain music teacher, best known for sporting a spotted bow tie and coiffure, being not dissimilar to her majesty the Queen's, seemed particularly interested in corporal punishment and whose motives for observing a thrashing I have always considered questionable. Then there was the R.E teacher, who was renowned for throwing the board duster, a solid block of wood, if you weren't paying attention, or the Science teacher, whose hands were like coal grabs and could leave you semi-concussed with one whack. I could go on … and on.

The sixth form common room was situated in the old hall with its sweeping staircase, brass door handles and oak panelled walls. The sixth form prefects had authority to issue lines to recalcitrant pupils and further punishment ensued if their orders were not fulfilled on time.

I recall that there was a corridor leading to the common room, which was about six feet wide, and that the light switches that served the corridor were made of brass. Someone – though how it was discovered is now lost in the mists of time – had ascertained that an electric current would pass through the body if the hands that held the switches were linked across the corridor. This came in very useful when terrorising first year pupils who could be given electric shocks as they walked past. By holding the switch then jabbing them in the neck, a significant amount of current would pass through the body. The only down side being that all parties involved in the prank were electrified at the same time, but as long as the initiative remained with the prefects then it was a trick worth repeating and remained a prank that would pass from one school year to the next.

Dicky Durrant was the school's Deputy Head. His facial features resembled that of a heavy weight boxer that had suffered years of punching above his weight and at the same time been ravaged by a life of heavy smoking. My first introduction to him was when we gathered on my first day of school with the rest of the apprehensive first years. I wore a peaked cap with a distinctive yellow banana shape at the back, new blazer, tie and short trousers and stood awkwardly with the new recruits. We had gathered in the quadrangle, which was surrounded by high wire fencing and 1950's styled, pre-fabricated school rooms. It felt, and looked, more like Colditz than a modern Grammar school.

A raised platform at the end of the quad served as a platform for Dicky Durrant, who now appeared, complete with mortar board, cloak and whistle. After glowering with murderous intent at the new entrants, he blew the whistle. The noise reduced a little but when not to his satisfaction he roared 'THAT MEANS SHUT UP.' Welcome to Moseley Hall.

By the age of 13, I was far more interested in spending time with the wayward youth of Moseley Hall Grammar School than in academia, and consequently my senior years in education were far more influenced by my miscreant piers, than my studies at Moseley Hall. This was reflected in the number of times I was found bent over Dicky Durrant's desk being thrashed.

In hindsight, a pivotal moment came at age 13, when I was top of my year in English. My English teacher had said, at the only parents evening where I ever received a good report, that I was set for a scholarship at Cambridge. I had written a book that year which had won the second year, literacy prize. Unfortunately a perfunctory teacher had lost it and shown a considerable lack of remorse in doing so. It had been something I had put my heart and soul into, with hand painted pictures and text that had been carefully typed. His dismissive attitude hit me hard and I was certain that if he couldn't be bothered – neither could I. It is certainly true that a good – or bad teacher can have a profound effect on pupils and influence subsequent outcomes that shape their future.

My elder brother Mike had been a star pupil, being fast tracked in the Alpha stream and straight off to Sussex University. The same could not have been said of me, or indeed my younger brother Andy as we competed for; 'the worst pupil's Moseley Hall has ever had,' according to the Deputy Head. Well, I guess the feeling was mutual. I left with three O-levels in English and one in metalwork, my younger brother gained just two O's.

Around 1970 a charismatic, American evangelist called Arthur Blessitt came to Manchester. Anyone who remembers him will recall he travelled around the world with a large wooden cross which he would erect wherever he was preaching, usually in busy town centres. During his UK tour he visited Cheadle St Mary's church, and my mother, Christine Hawthorne, acquired two tickets for the event. To my surprise one of my mates, Dave Hardy, was interested in going so I agreed to go with him. The church was packed, and as we arrived late we were given seats in the choir stalls. I believe Arthur Blessitt was the originator of the, 'Give us a J… give us an E… ' chant and handed out – Jesus Loves You stickers wherever he preached. His message was powerful and at the end, led to an appeal. Around 30 people put their hands up including, to my amazement, Dave Hardy, after which I followed. We were asked to pray, and then those who had put their hands up to go out to the front. Well, putting your hand up was one thing, but going to the front of a packed church was quite different. I remember Arthur clearly saying, 'It is really important that you come out tonight if you put your hand up,' obviously referring to us. But we were staying put.

Around about the same time my mum bought me his best selling book, called 'Turned On To Jesus.' I recall reading it, but remained unconvinced.

Only God knows how the following years would have shaped up for me if I had gone forward at that meeting but it was to be petty crime, drugs and drunkenness in the main that I would increasingly turn to. I feel it is important to record my wayward adolescent years honestly here in the hope that it may encourage other parents who suffer at the hands of children who have gone off the rails. Do not give up on them. Prayer does change things and it does change people though sometimes it takes persistence and patience in equal measure. I also hope that a testimony that has a bad start and a positive outcome reflects the grace offered by God, who is able to take all our rubbish and turn it into something good.

Pictures of me as an adolescent are few and far between but here's one of my first motor bike whilst leading my younger brother Andy astray in our back garden in Cheadle.

It was the mid 70's, and with easy access to drugs I was soon moving on from Marijuana to LSD. This drug is capable of some of the most mind-bending experiences imaginable, and though not addictive is dangerous in many other ways and a very bad trip as it is called, when I was 16, brought the habit to an end. My bad trip though may have been a mixed blessing because the awfulness of it scared me off drugs completely. I can remember the details of the event clearly; it was not uncommon to mix rat poison with LSD for reasons I am not aware of, but whatever the composition, it had a devastating effect. The next four hours turned into a nightmare of demonic proportions where I didn't know either who I was or what I was. I remember clearly that there was a theme running through my bad trip, of a great demonic battle (with Arthur Blessitt playing a central role), and a grid, that I took to be hell that I was being sucked into. Eventually I was taken to Wythenshawe hospital where, I have been told, two policemen held me down whilst I was tranquilised. I wonder if the spiritual context of this terrible experience was simply drug induced, resulted from a deep seated guilt that I had never lived up to my parents expectations, or was there some profound demonic battle for my soul taking place? I was unconscious for sometime and recall the doctor being relieved that I hadn't suffered brain damage. One may imagine that this would be a precursor to my appointment with faith, but that was not to be until some years later.

The staff of Moseley Hall left me in no doubt that my presence there was surplus to their requirements, and I left school at 17 with my paltry qualifications. My metal work O-level served as some assistance in panel beating the dents from the numerous car accidents that were to follow, but it would be a long time before I would put the English O-level's to use.

I persuaded my father, at this tender age, to lend me £90 to buy a 3.4 litre, Mark 2 Jag, which I had found for sale. In hindsight, it was one of the more foolish things he did for me and an engine that size in the hands of a testosterone-charged juvenile-delinquent was a potentially lethal weapon.

I had the first of 11 separate accidents in it, in the first month of ownership. I was travelling down Kingsway, now the A34, at 75 miles per hour, showing off to a friend, when a car pulled out. I swerved left to avoid it and demolished the two drivers-side doors of a taxi. I pulled over to examine the damage to my two-ton Jaguar and found it had no more than a slight dent in the wing. My dad naively accepted that it wasn't my fault and wrote a forceful letter to the Insurance Company, and I got off. The Mark 2 remains one of the most beautiful designs of car I have ever seen, and quintessentially English, but to me at the time; it was just a great way of pulling girls.

To go with my new image I had converted a starting pistol to fire real bullets. It was certainly capable of putting a hole in your leg or worse, and was kept in my glove compartment in true gangster style. It did look alarmingly authentic.

To keep a 3.4 litre engine fed, whilst I was on the dole, I resorted to petrol syphoning and was successful in running my Jag for several months on stolen fuel, before the police saw me one night in Cheadle car park. I calmly put the equipment in the boot of the car and drove off at a steady pace until they decided to pull me over on Schools Hill. I immediately put my foot down and turned right down Daylesford Crescent, and after a short, reckless and adrenalin-fuelled chase, lost them.

The following day I was spotted by the same Police car, and being understandably peeved for being given the slip, the policeman pursued me with flashing lights and siren blaring. Some madness took over me and I put my foot down and proved that the Constabulary Panda cars were no match for an idiot with a Jag.

My friend, Dave Hardy, had been left in charge of his house whilst his parents were away, so, having again lost the Police car, I headed there. However the Jag was spotted outside and within five minutes, seven Police cars raced to the scene as an alert had been put out for a gold-coloured Mark 2 Jag, driven by a moron. I had taken the gun inside and hidden it, and after a search of the vehicle and without me in it, there was nothing they could do but hope to catch me on some future misdemeanour.

A shunt in the back, one in the front and a large dent in the door to match the original one on the wing, meant the car looked as despairing as my parents. When the prop shaft finally seized on the Motorway at 90 miles per hour, sending a huge bar of metal hurling down the inside lane, the car was finally scrapped.

My mother had always claimed there was a demon under the bonnet but the demon was me, driven by some strange, self-destruct mechanism. I was in danger of heading for a life of crime and the inevitable, subsequent prison sentences. Having already received a conditional discharge for theft in a juvenile court I was high on the local Police radar. Perhaps it was only my parent's prayers that allowed me to escape a jail sentence.

Big collars and wide ties were a sure sign that these two brothers were destined for the fashion business.

I have long since made my peace with my father, who was a kindly man who loved his children but sadly died in 1990 at the age of just 62. He was gracious enough to forgive me long before. To my mother, who is still alive, thank you for those prayers that I hope you may continue to see in fruition.

I had a number of dead-end selling jobs before gaining better employment selling building fixings for a national company. After a training period at the head office at Royston in Hertfordshire, I was moved to the Leeds office where I shared a rented house. I was just 18 years of age but found that selling suited me and made reasonable progress. Within 18 months I was managing the Manchester sales office. This could have led to a genuine career opportunity, but when I was invited to join my friend Dave Hardy, who was to travel to the Canary Islands in search of work and then onto – well anywhere, the thought of such an adventure was too much to resist.

CHAPTER 2

THE CANARY ISLANDS

It is common to take exotic gap years today, but in the early 70's this was a proper adventure. We raised around £150 between us, and in November 1975 set off for France, on the first leg of our journey. We caught a lift with a friend returning to University in London, and from there we planned to hitch-hike the next leg.

By the end of the day, and with a number of fortuitously-thumbed lifts, we arrived at Dover ferry port. It was the first time I had ventured abroad, and as the ships propellers churned the water to froth and powered us from the harbour, I wondered how long it would be before I returned. That first experience of leaving the shores of England, and the sheer excitement of foreign travel was never to leave me.

Our first night was spent shivering in a park in Calais and waking to an inch of snow on our sleeping bags and bemused children on their way to school. There followed a demoralising day of waiting by the roadside in near freezing temperatures, and at the point where we were seriously thinking of giving up, we managed to thumb a lift from an Englishman in an old Bedford van bound for Toulouse. The man had recently bought a town house that he was renovating, but judging by his means of transport, he was less than affluent. The driver's side door was missing, and the consequent hole, had been filled with a sheet of plastic taped to the body which threatened to fly off if the speed increased much above 40 miles per hour. The heater had long since packed in and with a chilly wind blowing through the van, the solution was to climb into sleeping bags and share his flask of soup. Our spirits began to lift.

By Toulouse the weather had improved and the grey skies of England were soon replaced by the deep blue of the Riviera. We slept under a starlit sky on the beach at Canet-en-Roussilion and the following day crossed the border into Spain.

It took us a further three days to reach the Spanish port of Algeciras, where we had planned to get the ferry crossing to Gran Canaria. However we hadn't anticipated the 3rd class tickets being sold out, and we were faced with two, £50 second class tickets, or a months wait for the next ferry, and a cheaper crossing. With money being tight we considered hanging around on the beach for a while and getting the cheaper boat but reasoned we still had to eat so settled on the former option and set sail on a Spanish passenger ferry, bound for Las Palmas, the capital of Gran Canaria.

The year was 1975 and Queen was topping the charts with Bohemian Rhapsody and the night clubs were dancing to, 'I believe in miracles,' by Hot Chocolate.

Though there was a developed tourist trade in the mid 70's, it was a far cry from the modern Island resort that the Canary Islands are today. The port side was heaving with industry. Great piles of bananas, oranges and spices were being moved on hand-drawn carts or wrapped in capacious jute bags, full of all kinds of food and multifarious merchandise from Africa, which lay waiting for loading on the appropriate vessel. Every country I have ever visited has its own distinctive smell and the heat of an African sun combined with the port's cargo to make a heady mix.

We arrived to find that, during the period of our crossing, the Fascist dictator, General Franco had died. The Spanish police were decidedly agitated and aggressively wanting to stamp down on any unrest. In addition, a rag tag Moroccan army had invaded the Spanish Sahara, causing many to flee to the Canaries and taking up most of the bar work that we had hoped would earn us a modest living.

It was perhaps the first real opportunity to test my entrepreneurial skill, and as such invested in a new-technology, Polaroid camera and began to sell photos to wealthy German tourists. Many Germans found it cheaper, and more therapeutic to recover from an operation in The Canary Islands than in their home towns, and we considered a souvenir photo of their recuperation, using the latest technology, was just what they needed.

The camera cost around £20, and a film about £12. The first film came free, with 10 shots in it and we decided to test the first few photos on ourselves. The image emerged from the bottom of the camera as if by magic and, happy with the result, we set off for the beach. Having secured our first German clients by a method of gesticulation and a smattering of their language that Dave remembered, we took our first photos. Unfortunately – and I can offer no reasonable explanation why – when we took the next two shots the exposure didn't work. We retreated and I successfully took a shot of my friend Dave, and was relieved when the following photo was successful and a satisfied German handed over the equivalent of £2.00. The next paid customer was not as accommodating and insisted we reshoot him, which we did, and for which he paid £2.00. We celebrated with a beer and a sandwich each, then to our horror realised that we didn't have enough money for another film. There was nothing for it but to sell the camera at a significant loss, and rethink our business plan.

The solution came with the purchase of a crate of oranges, which the Germans also seemed fond of. Our elementary education came in handy and for the next few days our chant of 'Oranges, funf fur funzig peseta,' was to be heard from one end of the beach to the other. Things were going well and we were marketing our second crate when the Police arrived. We had been reported by a jealous bar owner, and were arrested for selling oranges without a license and confined to a Spanish police cell awaiting a translator.

Despite my contentions with her majesty's constabulary in England, this was the first time I had been behind bars and being in a foreign country and with an incomprehensible language, the situation was understandably alarming. The cell was no more than 10ft x 8ft with no beds and only a hole in the corner for a toilet. Dave also began to develop violent stomach cramps, probably due to our poor diet, and this and our surroundings meant that our mood was low.

The following day we were interrogated and to our relief then released, on the firm understanding that we would leave the island within one week. This was easier said than done as we hardly had enough money to eat, never mind travel.

A visit to the British Consulate confirmed that there was to be no bail out from that direction but local knowledge is always valuable on these occasions and we soon learned from some resident hippies that blood was in high demand, and one litre of my zero positive blood group could be exchanged for the princely sum of the equivalent of £20.00. We visited one Dr Ramirez, who we had been told would be interested in our corpuscles and following a simple blood test, we were escorted into his surgery.

To see a full litre of your own blood flow from a small tube in your arm, and into a glass jar is an interesting experience and one where you readily convince yourself that death will shortly follow. However, a pint of milk later we were feeling almost normal, and headed off to the local Smorgasbord restaurant to stuff ourselves. Our fortunes however, had not turned as substantially as we thought. We had opted to sleep rough on the beach, where we thought we had found a safe place to leave our belongings, but that evening we had our clothes and money stolen whilst visiting a church, and were left with nothing more than a sleeping bag, a passport and a few coins.

The church visit was not intended to be a religious experience, rather a cheap place to spend a few hours, but as the most beautiful music I had ever heard flowed from the choir stalls, I had an overwhelming desire to do what I saw as something good, and so gave the very last of our kitty money into the collection box on the way out. When I eventually told Dave, I was relieved to find that he seemed remarkably unconcerned at the fact that I had literally given away every peseta we had in the world, and, without consultation, had included his share of the kitty money.

Simple cash calculations and a limit to how much blood we could manufacture suggested that we were faced with the reality of phoning home for help. Relationships with my father had been strained before I left, and it was through gritted teeth that I eventually made a reverse-charge call home. My father refused the money for a flight, but instead cabled £45 for us to return by sea, and so we reluctantly began to consider our return journey.

The port of Gran Canaria was surprisingly lax in security, and we discovered it was easy to pass through the port gates and access the ships. We managed to climb the side of the vast bulk of a BP oil tanker to see if there was the possibility of a cheap crossing to the Persian Gulf – for no particular reason, but there were no takers. The immense size of the ship meant that we were walking the deck unspotted for a full fifteen minutes and seriously considered stowing away in one of the life boats. But we were unsure when the ship would sail, and had not come prepared with food for such a journey. We were eventually apprehended and escorted off the vessel. The trip to the port was not in vain however as we did discover that there was a small banana boat heading for Morocco on the African coast, and the fee for our passage seemed very reasonable.

CHAPTER 3

EL AYUN

Dave and I were aware that there had been some military scuffles in Morocco but having failed to fully understand the meaning of the word 'invasion,' we decided to return to England via the Spanish Sahara and travel up through Morocco and settled into our two bunks on the modest working vessel that was heading for the small, Arab town of El Ayun.

It is hard to remember much of the trip as my head was down the toilet for much of the choppy duration, but when we arrived at the port of El Ayun, we were greeted by a menacing group of armed soldiers who looked suspiciously at the newly arrived, teenage Westerners.

We soon learned that the Spanish had fled the town when the Moroccan army had arrived, and all routes out of the town were blocked. The primitive people of El Ayun seemed friendly enough, but as I had skipped Arabic at school and English being of little use to them, communication was primarily via hand signals. Quite why this is always mutually accompanied by the words anyway, when you know full well it isn't understood, I have never quite comprehended.

Women were scarcely seen in the town, apart from carrying out chores on their flat-roofed houses, and even then, with their faces covered from view. The men gathered in various places around the town, no doubt to discuss the recent, military developments, and to enjoy their deep brown tobacco, and even darker coffee. To a man they were clad in Jellaba, a sort of hooded cape that seemed to us surprisingly heavy for a desert climate.

It would have been helpful to have had more knowledge of the invasion before we sailed, but perhaps the ship's Captain was more interested in his passengers' cash than being forthcoming with this information. We found out later that it was the last cargo vessel to have been allowed into the port for some months. It was certainly too late for recriminations, and we could not stay in the town indefinitely as funds would not allow. It would also be some time before a vessel was returning to the Canary Islands, so we took the decision to avoid the army post on the edge of town, and head out across the desert, and rejoin the only road to the next town, Tan Tan, which, according to our map was around 10 miles away and situated across the border within Morocco. Of course, we wouldn't attempt this expedition without proper supplies, and so purchased a bottle of water, a loaf of bread and a bag of tomatoes from the local market, before settling down to a night under the African sky.

There are few places in the world today where you can escape the light pollution that impairs the view of the night sky. The desert is certainly one, and as the vast canopy of a myriad of stars opened above us it was hard to be homesick for the grey skies and routines of Manchester life. This was an adventure and one we didn't want to end any time soon.

Having avoided any curious onlookers we headed out in the early morning, from the east of the town, and so avoided the army check point. An hour's steady walking and El Ayun was out of sight. We found ourselves surrounded by nothing but sand, and an increasing, but unspoken reality, that what we were doing was decidedly unwise.

An hour passed as the midday desert heat increased and beads of sweat began to break out on our foreheads as the gritty sand resisted our progress. In the distance we spied, what looked to be a rubbish dump. On approaching, and after passing an alarming pile of bones, which we hoped was of sheep or goats; we stumbled upon a substantial pile of Spanish-army paraphernalia. It appeared that the soldiers had fled the town, leaving all their army gear, including kit bags, shirts, boots and gun belts at this spot. Feeling our fortunes were improving, and having had all our clothes stolen in the Canaries, we stuffed the kit bags with free clothes and replaced our own dirty clothes with that of a Spanish infantryman, complete with gun belt and boots. In hindsight, this wasn't the smartest thing to do in a war zone as the Moroccan Captain was later to point out, whilst waving a revolver at us.

After a further mile, and wondering if our kit bags would prove to be too heavy to complete the journey, a small fighter plane passed over head, followed shortly after by a helicopter that circled menacingly above us. Around 10 minutes later a truck was seen coming, from the general direction of El Ayun, creating a trail of dust from the desert sand, as it darted towards us.

As it approached, it was clear that we were in trouble, and as 10, heavily armed soldiers rushed at us, shouting and waving rifles, we were glad they arrested us, rather than finishing the job there and then. We were taken back to camp, and after convincing the Captain we were in fact foolish English teenagers, rather than Spanish deserters, we were once again placed in custody.

I considered pointing out that the text in the front of my passport states that 'Her Britannic Majesty's Secretary of State requests and requires in the name of Her Majesty to those whom it may concern to allow the bearer to pass freely without let or hindrance,' etc, etc, but it seemed unwise. It also turned out not to be necessary as the following day, and with the Captain keen to get rid of us, we were given an armed escort on the back of a lorry, as part of a convoy of vehicles that was heading for Tan Tan.

Our convoy consisted of an armed jeep at the front and rear and a series of decrepit lorries, conveying various types of merchandise that was no doubt to be traded in Tan Tan. I remember clearly that our particular vehicle had a large quantity of a known brand of chocolate spread, which suggested to me that El Ayun was not quite as isolated from the outside world as I had been led to believe.

The road along the Western Sahara ran parallel with an exquisite length of unspoilt beach, where the glistening white surf separated the ubiquitous sand and turquoise sea of the Atlantic Ocean, from the deep blue African sky. To our right was a vast expanse of inhospitable desert stretching far into the horizon.

Amazingly, and seemingly in the middle of nowhere, we would come across a single home where children played outside, and where there appeared to be nothing more than a few goats to support their family. That, and the occasional camel train was the only obvious sign of desert life, be that animal or vegetable. There were however, more flies than one would imagine it was possible for the desert to sustain, in view of the lack of visible rotting matter for them to hatch from. On the one occasion we were forced to stop it was only seconds before every lightly coloured surface became covered in them, all keen to get some meagre sustenance from our convoy.

The train of vehicles had slowed and the Captain in the escort vehicle waved back excitedly to the attendant wagons, and shouted something in Arabic. The column of vehicles followed the lead jeep off the road and onto the desert sand as it tentatively picked its way past an upturned lorry. A load of fresh fruit was distributed in a 10 yard radius around the mangled undercarriage. A large crater in the road identified that the lorry had inadvertently driven over a land mine and the unfortunate driver had stood little chance of surviving the blast. In later life, such an event would be alarming, but to two 19 year old adventurers this was excitement of the highest order. In any case we judged that the Captain's vehicle at the front of the convoy would be as good a mine detector as we needed for the rest of our desert passage.

Our journey ended too swiftly but the delights of Tan Tan were not to disappoint. A camel market was being held, fringed by market stalls with every type of food that was offensive to an English pallet. Vulture, lizard, goat's heads and plates of offal of unidentified origin were intermingled with spices, vegetables, fruits and more vultures. The smell, mainly of camel, and the vigorous haggling combined with the trader's vocal advertising, left the senses tingling.

A large, tin pan of white liquid caught our eye and we enquired from a trader as to what it may be. 'Is yogit,' he replied gruffly. This seemed safer than many of the other delicacies being offered so we sampled a cup of what turned out to be literally sour milk, which to the vendors amusement we quickly spat out, but then we couldn't really argue or request a refund – that is, after all, what yoghurt is.

The night was spent under the stars and the following day we were able to negotiate a passage on the back of another wagon, heading north, where we descended at Agadir. This was long before the town became a popular holiday resort and we managed to negotiate a bed for the night for no more than a few British shillings. We ordered a very acceptable omelette and drank sweet mint tea as we watched the sun melt into the Atlantic Ocean. The following day we caught a bus that doubled up as a sheep, goat and vegetable courier bound for the coastal town and port of Tangiers.

It was Christmas day and we celebrated with marmalade sandwiches, which was the nearest thing to British food we could find in the supermarket and all we felt our meagre budget would allow. A glass of beer completed our festive meal.

The bustling souks and crowded coffee bars of Tangiers seemed to be under a permanent fog of hookah pipes and marijuana fumes, and even the Police seemed to be smoking dubious, hand-rolled cigarettes. It wasn't long before we were approached by a dealer who held out, apparently without any concern of reprisals from the authorities, the largest block of dope we had ever seen. The price was £15 and we considered it too much of a bargain to refuse, reckoning that we could sell it for four times that much back in England. There must be many thousands of young people, idling in jails around the world, following one similar, single act of reckless folly. It was only by the greatest good fortune that we didn't join them.

We passed easily through Moroccan customs with the block of marijuana bulging down the front of my trousers and boarded a ferry for mainland Spain. It wouldn't have taken much imagination to judge that Spanish customs would be more zealous, especially following the death of General Franco a month earlier, but thinking sensibly was a gift we had yet to develop. To our alarm, we saw that all bags were being searched on entry but surprisingly the body wasn't. A sniffer dog would have picked up our scent from a considerable distance – but fortuitously there were none to be seen. We passed through with our contraband undetected, and as a fine drizzle suggested it was likely to be persistent, we sought free accommodation and spent the night in a concrete mixer.

The following day brought fine weather and we began the long journey home by hitching a ride with a Spanish family. The parents spoke good English and enjoyed our story as we relayed our adventures across the Sahara. It was only when we were explaining that we intended to hitch down to Calais and return via the ferry that we realised that we wouldn't have enough money for the crossing. The thought of phoning our parents to ask for help again was an unbearable failure we weren't prepared to concede. The couple enthusiastically suggested we consider trying our luck in Gibraltar: 'There is a lot of work there we hear. It is very difficult for the Spanish with the border being closed, but two English young men should have no problem.'

This seemed like an excellent suggestion and we would have just enough money to get the short ferry crossing back to Morocco, then onto Gibraltar from there. We thanked them for their advice as they dropped us off at the next road junction.

The spectacular foolishness of again, taking a large piece of an illegal drug through a Fascist customs post, stuffed down the front of our trousers, still leaves me with a rush of anxiety. Just how long we would have been held in prison for doesn't bear thinking about but the eyes of the Police were diverted as they once again searched our bags. It is also surprising that they didn't recognise that our kit bags were full of Spanish army apparel. It may be a fluke that we were not apprehended then, but as we passed through the ambivalent Moroccan border post, only having to face the far more zealous, British one, we felt we were seriously pushing our luck. The British Customs were manned by Policemen in very familiar uniforms but one look at our passports and we passed through with our illicit hoard and entered the British governed, Rock of Gibraltar.

Perhaps I should pause for a moment and remind the reader and indeed myself, why I have recorded my story in this way. During the 1970's and 80's there was a tendency in evangelical circles to look for exciting testimonies, and converted bank robbers and drug dealers were in high demand. Books such as Run Baby Run, which told the story of Nicky Cruz and his gang life in Brooklyn, were best sellers. This may be less true today and I hope that I will not raise too many eyebrows by being honest about my own story. We can read how Paul the apostle approved of the death of Stephen – an innocent man – and in Acts 8:3 we read that he; 'began to destroy the church. Going from house to house, he dragged off men and women and put them in prison.' His subsequent conversion is all the more powerful because of the life he had left behind. I hope that the foolishness of my own past may be seen in the same way.

It is hard to imagine quite how annoying it must be for the Spanish to have something which is so clearly a part of Spain, yet ruled by the British. I wonder how we would feel if the Great Orme or Land's End was under say, German or French rule.

With the Spanish border being closed, Gibraltar had become a Mecca for alcohol enthusiasts, with 365 bars on a 7 square kilometres stretch of land, literally one bar for every day of the year. The term 'rock happy' was often used in connection with the many hundreds of hitch-hikers who had made it to Gibraltar and stayed on, almost permanently inebriated on cheap, Caribbean rum. Their tipple of choice was titled 151 Rum, which was purported to relate to the degrees of alcohol and had been known to send people blind.

We booked in at a cheap hostel that was mainly patronised by Arabs who were benefitting from the mini building boom taking place. We quickly learned of a British company that was recruiting. The following day we managed to locate the offices of the business and were interviewed by a middle aged English man who seemed more curious about the recent adventures of these two enterprising back packers, than their qualifications in construction. We were duly hired as labourers on £30 a week, and placed under the supervision of Mario, the company foreman.

The builders were completing a high rise office block and our initial task was to remove debris from the top floor and generally tidy up. However, after a week or so the menial jobs there dried up and we were trusted with greater responsibility. Mario needed some foundations laying for a new beach bar and we were trusted with the job of digging an eight by four metre hole in the sand and installing shutters prior to concrete foundations being laid. Mario was primarily focused on completing the high rise to a tight deadline, and with virtually no instruction and nothing more that two spades and some shutters, we were left to use our initiative.

Now anyone who has experienced the delights of building sand castles and advancing to digging holes on the beach will recall that sand is inherently unstable, and the excavated sides of a hole have a habit of caving in. After two weeks of wrestling with the shutters and no sign of Mario, and nothing more to show for our labours than a well developed sun tan, we assumed he must have forgotten about us. We decided that beach life suited us well and it seemed a shame to spoil it by asking for assistance. It was a full three weeks before Mario got round to checking up and after uttering a number of unfamiliar Spanish expletives, went off to organise a JCB. The hole took about a further 30 minutes to dig.

Following our misdemeanour with the beach hut we were henceforth more closely supervised. Mario though was an amiable chap, and seemed to like us. We took to calling him 'Uncle Mario,' and asking if we could borrow his car for the weekend to tour the Rock. I still remember his terse reply; 'there are two things I never lend, my car … and my wife.'

The company secured a contract to replace a strip of tarmac at the Airport and Dave and I joined a team of eight other men with the task of ripping the old surface out with a pneumatic drill. The airport combined military flights with civilian and we grew to look forward to the fighter jets turn to leave the runway then launch near vertically into the sky fired by white hot thrusters.

The drill was surprisingly heavy and combined with such aggressive jarring to the bones that we wondered if Mario was getting his own back for our beach fiasco. My days on the runway were cut short when I tried to lift the drill improperly and pulled my back out. I was a good two weeks in bed and on pain killers before I was any use to the building trade again.

When I eventually felt that I too was in danger of becoming 'rock happy,' and having saved enough money to fly home, I bought a one way ticket with British Airways – my first ever experience of aviation. I arrived back on the 5th April having been away for exactly six months, though Dave stayed on for a further six weeks. The joy of foreign travel and the excitement of discovering new and exciting destinations have never left me, even after 38 countries and over 1000 flights, though my fondness of airports has long waned.

The bible talks about predestination and free will as if they are intertwined. For example in the book of Acts 2 v 23 it states that Jesus death was 'by the predetermined plan and foreknowledge of God.' Yet the book of Mathew records Jesus prayer in 26 v 39 – 'Going a little farther, he fell with his face to the ground and prayed, "My Father, if it is possible, may this cup be taken from me. Yet not as I will, but as you will."' Jesus had the choice to avoid the cross and wrestled with that choice. It is difficult to understand how the two – freewill and predestination – can both be possible, but that is clearly what the bible indicates. As I look back on my own life I see how much God was reaching out to me as He is reaching out to all of us. Like Michael Angelo's famous and remarkable image of God – straining to reach out to a relaxed and indifferent Adam, as portrayed on the Sistene Chapel in Rome. Through all my wickedness I see how God was reaching out to me. Once His hand was taken – He recycled all of the bad – and the good to a better outcome. I see how my experiences in my early life have shaped my present and influenced my business life. I hope that my story may encourage you to pray for your loves ones, as they may from time to time go astray. I am also convinced that prayer engages God in the abstruseness of our predestined path.

My father, George Hawthorne, had been a journalist for 30 years, having worked for many years on the Manchester Evening News, before taking a more aspirational job on the Manchester Guardian. Having worked his way up to Deputy News Editor, a combination of the stress of the job and little interest in material possessions, had persuaded him to take early redundancy. My mother, Christine had impressed and surprised us all in equal measure when, with her child rearing duties behind her, she studied, then qualified as a primary school teacher. As I returned from my travels, the sale of the Cheadle family home was well advanced and my parents bought a six acre small holding in mid Wales where my father could indulge his eccentricities, and as he suggested, 'opt out.'

I enjoyed a brief spell helping them move in and redecorate a converted mill house in an idyllic spot in mid Wales, with 700 feet of fishing rights on the River Banwy. My stay though was cut short, when I received a phone call from a friend of mine, John Wilcox, who was looking for a labourer to help him ruin perfectly good houses with the application of imitation stone cladding. It was a new fad where admirably decent brick was disguised as stone by embellishing it with reconstituted and dyed, sand tiles. You may have seen a blue version on Coronation Street, embellishing the Duckworth's home. Perhaps our greatest crime was in the case of high quality stock brick which had a particularly smooth finish. It was our practice to cut great grooves in the brick face with a stone cutter to gain greater purchase. In the event that the fashion for cladding ended, which it soon did, the damaged brick had to be rendered, the beautiful Stock Brick lost for all time. For all those who suffered at our hand, I am deeply penitent.

*All who visited my parents at the old Mill would vouch for
the warm hospitality they received.*

With nowhere to stay, John offered me a bed for a couple of days with his mother and himself, at their home in Heald Green. I was still there two years later. Our trade took us all over Greater Manchester, in search of people without a shred of taste or financial competence. Soon our skills extended to sand blasting, where we frosted several windows before realising we needed to cover them and famously renamed the

Victoria Pub, the 'ic Pu,' by destroying the expensive signage. When the wind caught the scaffolding tower one day and, aided by castors, a 20ft high construction took off down the high street, nearly killing one of our employees who was spread eagled on top, we took up plastering. No job offer was rejected, and as long as the finish was accepted as stippled, even if the client had originally commissioned smooth, we progressed. Woodwork likewise was attempted as it is amazing how even large gaps can be hidden with wood filler. It was a long time ago, but I again feel the need to apologise, and to all whose fate was to employ us, I am deeply repentant.

Most of our ill-gotten earnings were spent in the Conway pub, a tasteless 70's establishment frequented by under age drinkers. At closing time we would head off in our silk bowling shirts and ridiculously highly-wasted trousers, with 40 inch bottoms, to The Wigan Casino, an all-night Northern Soul Club, and dance until closing time at 7.00am. Our musical loyalties shifted with the emergence of the punk movement and weekends were spent at the Electric Circus in Manchester watching the Sex Pistols, The Stranglers, The Damned and the like. Another favourite haunt for us was The Ranch, Manchester's first punk venue, which was located on Dale Street in a corner of Foo Foo's Palace. We would hang out with Punk bands Magazine and The Buzzcocks that often visited the Ranch.

On the odd occasion that my parents returned to Cheadle, they would discover that my hair was coloured anything from bright orange to navy blue, and I made extensive use of the ubiquitous safety pins, being, for reasons I am unsure of, the chosen accessory of every true punk. Having played the electric guitar for some time I now aspired to join the newly emerging plethora of punk bands, being spat at on stage.

But then, against all the odds my life changed. It was transformed, remade, ripped apart with an authentic, 'road to Damascus,' spiritual experience.

CHAPTER 4

FINDING FAITH

My bedroom at number 68 Rossendale Road, Heald Green, was a small box room, just wide enough to allow you to get out of a single bed without crashing into the opposite side of the room. The house lacked central heating and in winter the ice was often layered thickly on the inside of the window. In the month of March, when I was 20 years old and for no particular reason I can recollect, I had a series of very unpleasant nightmares. They were demonic in nature in that they featured ghoulish and supernatural characters. For several nights in a row I would wake up perspiring with anxiety. I could have been offered a whole host of physical or mental reasons for the experiences, due to some recent or past excess, but the experiences remained deeply disturbing. One Monday night I awoke with my face to the wall, following a particularly unpleasant dream. Behind me, though I could only see him in my mind's eye, stood a man who was darker than the night. Though I fully realise this can be dismissed by a cynic as an extension of my vivid imagination, I was totally convinced of his reality and it was as real as if I was staring at him in broad daylight. My spine froze in terror and I was unable to move. All I could think to do was recite the Lord's Prayer that had been implanted deep into my memory from a hundred distant church services or school assemblies. I prayed, though I was not aware it was a prayer, and the image left.

John and I had bought a Bedford van, with which to carry out our construction catastrophes, and on one Tuesday in March, having finished work for the day, I was driving the van to visit my girl friend Lesley Rice, at her home in Cheadle Hulme. Throughout the journey the images from the dreams haunted me. My thoughts centred on the devilish character that I hoped would never reappear. What if it was real? What if there really is something as evil in this world as that person seemed to me? What then if there was a God? Would that make a difference? The thoughts were tormenting my mind. As I drove toward the traffic lights at Finney Lane I spoke, as if to God. 'If you are real I want to know you, if not I don't want to think of you again.' Though I confess it was not particularly profound, it was as genuine a prayer as I could muster, though I didn't think of it in that way at the time. But almost immediately I sensed a bubbling in my stomach. The bubbles rose up across my chest, and then to my neck until they reached my eyes and I burst into tears. The van was filled with the presence of something so lovely and wonderful, yet so powerful that I knew it was real. Though I couldn't see through the floods of tears, I knew there was the physical presence of a man that I took to be Jesus. I was wrecked and rejoicing in equal measure, at what I had found, what I felt and what I knew.

The van continued through the lights and turned left and then parked as if on autopilot. I remember clearly that I was shaking and crying so hard that I really do not think I had been in control of the vehicle. The experience was so utterly authentic and unsolicited as to be impossible to ignore.

After a while I recovered and drove the rest of the journey to my girl friend's house. As she answered the door I felt compelled to recount my experience exactly as it had happened. To my amazement she listened with genuine interest, then, to my further astonishment told me that she had been thinking about Jesus that week as well and had bought a book at a second hand book shop. Leslie went upstairs at once to retrieve it from her bedroom. I immediately recognised the book and the author – it was, Turned On To Jesus, by Arthur Blessitt.

'My mum bought me that book when I was about fourteen,' I said, taking it from her. I opened it and inside the front cover were written the words, 'To Simon, love mum.' It was the same book that my mum had bought me at the time I put my hand up when Arthur Blessitt had visited Cheadle. It was clear that someone was on my case and not going to go away.

Arthur Blessitt travelled over 40,000 miles and 321 countries in six decades carrying a wooden cross and preaching the Good News of the message of Jesus.

The experience had affected me so dramatically that I had no reservation at all in telling my mates what had happened to me. It didn't occur to me that I had become a Christian, just that I had met God. Nor did I know any other Christians, apart from my parents who now lived in Wales and I was keen to try and find someone who would understand or maybe explain what was going on. I called them and when my mother answered told her exactly what had happened to me. As she listened in silent amazement, she stopped me and ran over to the bookshelf. When she returned she was as amazed as I had been. 'I was sure that book was in my bookshelf.' she said. To this day we have no idea how it came to be in a second hand book shop on the High Street, five years after I had been given it.

I was convinced that I would have to become a vicar or something equally radical in restititution for my past discretions. In the first instance though, I thought I should attend church, and with the only one I had ever visited regularly as a child was Cheadle St. Mary's, I chose there.

I arrived at 6.00pm, assuming that was when the service would start, whilst casting a sheepish look over my shoulder in the direction of the White Hart pub situated next door, in case any of my mates had seen me. In fact I was 30 minutes early and as I entered a lone figure stood in the centre of the church, where the aisles joined to make the shape of a cross. He steered me, complete with navy blue hair, safety pins, leather jacket and a distinct sense of discomfort, to the very front row where I sat quietly for 30 minutes. In retrospect, the man, who I later discovered was called Alistair Carmichael, had inadvertently stopped me from leaving as there is no question that once the service began I would have legged it sharpish if I'd have had the chance. By the close of the service, which could have been in Mandarin for the sense it made to me, I had firmly committed myself to never darkening their doors again, but a young man named Mike Ward recognised me from our school days and insisted I go to a youth event at the Upper Room across the High Street. Though I continued to feel that I had entered completely unfamiliar territory, I was at least with people of my own age group. One of them was Ian Beeston, a bass player I also knew from my days at Moseley Hall. As we talked, and knowing that I played the guitar, he told me of a band he played in called the Bill Mason Band that was looking for a new lead guitarist. Probably out of pity at my obvious discomfort, in these decidedly unworldly surroundings, he invited me to an audition.

Paul the Apostle writes in the book of Acts of his 'road to Damascus experience.' Throughout the book of Acts he refers back to this time as his personal testimony and witness of the reality of his experience. He faces a Centurion guard and gives his testimony. Again in front of Governor Felix, and then Festus he tells of this experience. In front of King Agrippa, despite being ridiculed, he again tells his story, and then onto Caesar in Rome to plead his case. My own experience was, in its own way, not dissimilar to Paul's in that he too was an unlikely candidate for conversion and, though I knew nothing at that time of the book of Acts, I likewise felt compelled to tell my story to anyone that would listen. This, like Paul's experience, led to a fair amount of ridicule in the pub and a fair amount of disdain from my house mate John. However, it is the case I think, that genuine passion is attractive to some at least, and gradually a number of my friends softened. My younger brother Andy was fighting his own struggle to ignore the events of my conversion and about six months later, came to find God in his own way.

Later that year we visited the Keswick Convention together, a large Christian gathering in the heart of the beautiful Lake District. Our mother was also attending and had invited us, and when we met up she introduced us to an old lady called Olive Clark, who had retired there from Cheadle, some years earlier. Though I didn't recollect it then, she had apparently attended Cheadle St. Mary's many years before. 'I have prayed for you two boys every Saturday for the last 8 years,' she said.

I was amazed that someone could maintain that level of commitment to people that she would no longer regularly see, and indeed may never meet again. Her powerful and persistent prayers, combined with that of my mother's had created a force that I believe had made it impossible to resist and, if there is a God, as I chose to believe there is, and prayer is one of His principle methods of engagement with us, then it had enabled Him to move in our lives in ways I had previously never imagined could be possible.

As I have studied the mystery of prayer over the years since these events, I have come to realise that God took an incredible risk with mankind. The Bible indicates that God's purpose for all mankind was that He wanted a people that would, by freedom of choice, choose Him, a people that without coercion or bullying, would wish to develop a relationship on earth that would lead to an eternal relationship in heaven. It was always to be for His sake, as well as for our own. That relationship, which we know as salvation, is free, and freely rejected, and woven within the mystery of free will and God's divine foreknowledge of all that is, and was, and has yet to happen, it remains that prayer really does change things.

CHAPTER 5

THE BILL MASON BAND

The Bill Mason Band, with the exception of Bill, was a legacy from local bands, Apple Crumble and Cornerstone. Phil Holmes, Bill's flat mate, was keyboard player in both of these before being spotted by Word Music's Norman Miller and co-opted into the Alwyn Wall Band that went on to tour America. Other bands that emerged from the various group's musicians were 100% Proof and The Predators, fronted by the very individual Kev Smith.

My audition with the band was to be at St. Andrew's Methodist church in Wythenshawe, at the back of which, Dave Rawding, the drummer, had a flat with his wife Joy. Bill Mason, the vocalist, recalls that he took one look at this navy haired punk and wondered what on earth Ian was thinking of. It is also true to say that, listening to the decidedly wet songs that the band played at this time, we did in deed appear to be an unlikely match. However Bill was keen to develop the music and was strangely drawn to my aggressive guitar style and it was not long before we were rehearsing a new set to be unleashed on the unsuspecting church.

Christian music in the 1970's, not to be confused with Gospel music, had made a faltering attempt to become more contemporary than the likes of Pat Boone, and where Larry Norman and Andrea Crouch had made some inroads, we were keen to blaze a trail into genuine musical credibility. That said, we were self quoted as saying that 'most Christian Music is six years behind – we are just six months behind.'

One particular group, called the Movement Band, fronted by the highly charismatic Mike Hook, had developed a regular circuit of gigs and we found ourselves supporting them on several occasions. Mike was a Baptist minister with a pony tail and wore a massive cross as he roared into the microphone. The band had played together for a good few years and when they finally split we found ourselves taking over the circuit of gigs that they had developed.

After the Movement Band came to an end, their guitarist, Mick Spratt had been asked to put a P.A. together for a mission in Manchester called the Whole Story, with David Watson. A local solicitor and one of the organisers, Val Grieve, knew that Mick had kept hold of the bands P.A. and, after hiring a bit of gear in, he and Mike Hook had their first commercial rental for what was to become the foundation of Wigwam Acoustics, one of the industries finest and most respected P.A. companies who have gone on to work with the very top names in the music industry. In addition Mick has become one of my very favourite people on the planet ... and is also very handy if you need some P.A. gear.

The Christian music scene was keen to progress its credibility in the world's eyes, and after only a couple of gigs in local churches we found ourselves at the Greenbelt Festival in Bedfordshire, playing to 5000 people, along with fellow punk bands Giantkiller and the far more successful After The Fire. The following year, when Cliff Richard headlined, which coincided with his number one hit, 'We don't talk anymore' topping the charts, we played, knee trembling, on the the main stage on Saturday night to an audience of 20,000 people. Shortly afterwards we recorded our one and only album, No Sham, which we launched at the Salford Universities, Maxwell Hall in 1979.

Greenbelt was a great shop window for the band and we soon found ourselves travelling the country to play anywhere from a

University campus to a church youth group. We frequented glue sniffing clubs in Saint Helens and schools in Glasgow and always with an uncompromising Gospel message from Bill accompanied by our own style of musical attack.

Not long after the launch of our album, Phil Holmes fell in love with an amazing vocalist, Paula Grack, in Erie Pennsylvania whilst touring America with the Alwyn Wall Band. They got married the following year and Bill went over to be best man. Bill promptly fell in love with Carrie Koos, Paula's cousin, and they too were soon married. Initially Carrie moved to be with Bill in the U.K. but never really settled and when Bill finally decided to move to America it was the end of the band and our plans to go full time.

Love was certainly in the air and I was becoming increasingly interested in a colourful brunette named Julia. She had been part

Christians and Punk Rock were an unusual combination in the 1980's and the Bill Mason Band raised a few eyebrows amongst some conservative evangelicals.

of a wider crowd of girls that had been involved with the various bands that had emerged from South Manchester and, when Bill returned from America and we formed a house church, in association with Paula's church in Erie, we began to see a lot more of each other. It was an unnecessarily intense period for us all as we tried to understand the responsibilities of church leadership whilst still in our early 20's. The lack of a wiser elder to counsel us meant that we mistook spirituality for being a bit of a pratt on a few occasions.

My new found 'holiness,' also possibly influenced from a vast amount of philandering before I became a Christian, made me very shy of asking Julia out. After a month of praying about it I eventually asked one of the American elders for their guidance. 'Why don't you just ask her?' he said looking at me as if I was completely stupid. So I did, and soon found out that she had been feeling exactly the same way. Perhaps the lesson hadn't really been learned though, as I fasted for three weeks before asking her to marry me. No seriously, I really did.

The Bill Mason Band's uncompromising commitment to promote the Christian message would ensure that we would never have had financial success, but strangely and indirectly the band was to ensure that came to me in another way.

CHAPTER 6

INTO BUSINESS

At one of our gigs, whilst playing at Manchester University, we were supported by an acoustic guitarist named Nick Stone. Nick was a member of the Jesus Family, who were a community church in South Manchester. Nick supported himself by manufacturing leather belts but believed his future lay in glass blowing. He had one customer in the now defunct Oasis underground market on Market Street, who bought a steady quantity of a fashionable leather belt that Nick made. Nick needed help to complete an order and as I was in need of cash, I agreed to give him a hand.

Within a week, I had not only completed the order for Nick, but mastered the basic skills of making the belts. It made sense for me to carry on this modest business, which was carried out in a third floor room, not dissimilar to Fagin's lair, and in reality positioned above a pet shop in Ashton-Under-Lyne. This made the handling of cow hides difficult as we ascended the stairs and with nothing more than a few hand tools to work the leather, it was a modest enterprise indeed.

Nick did indeed leave to pursue a career in glass blowing and I was left to continue his work on my own. My first venture into business wasn't helped by not having a driving license, having lost it for driving without due care and attention. Though God is willing to forgive us, unfortunately the British judiciary are not always so forthcoming. So my orders were delivered by bus, to an ever increasing number of retailers in the North West. I moved the business to the 3rd floor of an old brick warehouse off Rochdale Road in the centre of Manchester. The building was owned by the Polish Krupa brothers, and their ancient father who, to the best of my knowledge, spoke no more than two words of English. The rent, rates, light and heat, were a very modest £15.00 a week, with no extra charge for the plethora of advice they were keen to give me.

Within twelve months I was experiencing the inevitable dichotomy of running a business as a one man band. Whilst I was selling, there was no manufacturing taking place and vice versa. I thought the solution may be found in my brother Andy, who had a job with a timber company. If I recall correctly he had progressed from banging nails into wood, and doing nothing else, to selling within the same firm. In any case, and with a little arm twisting, he joined me, just as nylon belts came into fashion. The simplest of manufacturing processes was then earning us £700 a week, a tidy sum then, in view of our modest overheads.

One of the mixed blessings of the fashion trade is that, by the very nature of its commodity, its life span is unpredictable and often short. Hence, the likes of nylon belts must be replaced with new product on a continuous basis. This leads to high excitement and potential rewards that can often be followed by the exact opposite.

We moved again to a modern unit on Store Street, and expanded our staff to six, whilst developing our product range into various leather and leather board belts, and even braces. Yes, we were a belts and braces business.

Our customer base increased to supplying a few multiples, like Chelsea Girl, who later became River Island, Dorothy Perkins and Top Shop, and we felt set for further expansion. We had traded as Nick Stone Accessories but considered a new name was appropriate and Andy suggested Hothouse, which stayed with us from then on.

We had supplied a few gentlemen's outfitters with braces, and Bobby Ball, of Cannon and Ball fame, helped in some part to boost sales of 'Rock on Tommy' braces. Yes, I know … but we needed the work. However, when Lady Diana was seen wearing a pair of braces, things took a significant step forward and the demand for our products increased. We quickly outgrew our premises and purchased a factory unit in Longsight. Within the next 12 months we were to make half a million pairs of braces and reward ourselves with an Audi Quatro and a Mercedes 500. However, our recruitment policy had yet to be developed and the need for new recruits was urgent. One obvious source for new employees is the job centre, but we hadn't realised quite how desperate the Longsight office was to place people on their books.

In the short time that we had acquired our new premises in Longsight, Manchester City Council, under pressure to reduce the crime rate in Moss Side, had moved the worst offenders onto our adjoining council estate. It wasn't long before our new neighbours had gleaned that the product we produced was easily disposed of for cash, in the local pubs. The first of many break-ins occurred, and after the second claim in three months, our insurance company became understandably tetchy. They insisted we have grills put over the windows and after the third claim, shutters over the grills.

We had always employed males in the factory as the work was reasonably heavy, and continued this policy with Longsight job centre. This would no doubt be considered discriminatory now, but quite how an eight stone girl is expected to handle a full cow hide of leather, I am not sure.

On one occasion, following a break in, the CID paid us a visit. We were explaining how we believed the thieves had gained access when the officer looked through the office window and into the factory. 'That's Neville Jolly,' he said. We agreed it indeed was and informed him that the job centre had sent him. Without another word the officer walked into the warehouse and immediately arrested him without so much as a caution. After remanding him in custody, he then called at the Jolley's family home, without a warrant, and retrieved several hundred pairs of braces from the loft. We were slightly red faced when he returned with the stolen goods and confessed we were also employing his younger brother.

In total we had 30 young men in production lines, and at least half came from the Longsight and Rusholme area, and each of them represented areas of deprivation from Manchester's inner city. It was this group of young men that were about to affect our lives in a remarkable way.

CHAPTER 7

THE MESSAGE

Andy and I had received a reasonable education, though we would be the first to admit we had abused it. We also had loving parents and a stable home life, but the more we got to know our new employees, the more we understood the deep social divide that existed within our city. In addition we came to understand that our staff knew absolutely nothing about the faith that had so massively influenced almost every part of our nation's heritage. They had never been to Sunday school, or church, unless it was to a wedding or funeral, and had received no religious education that had any meaning to them whatsoever – Jesus was an expletive, and no more.

We also knew that, in the main, the church in Manchester was spectacularly ill equipped to offer anything that they would relate to. There are always exceptions, and many wonderful people who would sincerely try, but as a collective group, the church in Manchester was woefully lacking in relating to the inner city, youth culture. In fact, in the 80's, Youth for Christ had recorded Manchester as being the nations toughest city to crack. How would the church ever overcome this obstacle?

In April 1987 we took a stand at the Harrogate Fashion Fair and in a quiet period began to talk about the issue of communicating something of the relevance of Christianity with our staff, in a contemporary way to which they would relate. As we talked we began to get more and more excited about the idea of kick-starting something ourselves. We had some financial resources through the business. We had contacts in music. We also knew enough people to at least try and do something relevant. We discussed booking Manchester's top rock venue – the Apollo theatre – for a week, and employing the most cutting edge musicians and entertainers that we could muster. In the space of a few minutes it seemed that we had downloaded the beginnings of a plan. It is strange to think that in 1987 very few people had access to computers, and we had never literally downloaded anything, so if for that reason alone, I will claim that our download was from God.

We later described our journey home to be as if we were flying. The sense of assurance that we were to attempt something original and authentic was stimulating and exciting. That evening Andy opened his bible at Isaiah 43 v 19. He read, 'See, I am doing a new thing! Now it springs up, do you not perceive it?' That same desire to stay at the cutting edge was to remain with the ministry that was to emerge, for the next 20 years.

Without any qualifications, other than enthusiasm, we knew that we were in need of endorsement and sought the approval of an esteemed group of church leaders within an organisation called ECMA, the Evangelical Council for the Manchester Area. Val Grieve arranged a slot at the next group meeting and we presented our case to a curious group of church elders. They were gracious enough to ignore our sharp suits with enormous collars. On reflection we did indeed look like a couple of spivs, but we emerged with a green, or at least amber light, and at least two elders firmly on board.

On January the first we launched our campaign at the Free Trade Hall and began our drive to recruit 400 churches in what was to be the largest youth mission ever to take place in Manchester. The main event was to be held for one week at the Apollo in October and we formed a steering group of Mick Spratt from Wigwam, Frank

Green, who was a youth pastor at Ivy Cottage before becoming their minister, Steve Goddard who would take on the media role and Mark Elder, who is now Senior Minster at Heaton Baptist Church in Newcastle. In addition we recruited link people in each of the ten boroughs of Manchester who would work with the local church. One of these was the amazing Paul Gibbs who went onto form the PAIS project which now employs 100's of people in over 8 countries. Paul Morley, an Assemblies of God evangelist was recruited to head up the street work.

Unsure of what to call the event, I was driving past the Apollo one day when I noticed that the band, The Mission was playing. It seemed an interesting name for a band and I wondered if we could plagiarise it, but then The Message came to mind and we all agreed it seemed appropriate.

We came within a sniff of getting Simon Mayo, who had been newly appointed as a Radio 1 DJ, to MC the evening, but Peter Powell, his manager at that time overruled on the grounds that associating with Christian events was commercial suicide. We instead recruited Scouse poet Steve Henderson, who now occasionally appears on BBC, Radio 4. We also managed to book Gloria Gaynor, Paul Jones, former vocalist with Man Fred Man's Earth band, and David Grant, along with Mike Peters from The Alarm who were having chart success at the time. We commissioned a stage set that resembled Coronation Street and drama group Riding Lights, who specially wrote a series of sketches for the week based around a fictional Manchester family – the Arkles. Over the week we had 17,000 people come through the doors and the largest number of coaches to ever visit the Apollo on one night. 1000 people made a first time commitment to Christ and on the Sunday night we closed with a celebration service with Graham Kendrick. We did indeed feel we had much to celebrate.

The event and build up had cost around £100,000 to stage and there remained around £15,000 of outstanding debt. The money dribbled in over the next few weeks from various donations, but a final £5000 stubbornly refused to be met. I recall someone taking us on one side in the early days of The Message and telling us how his own venture into ministry had cost him his house. We looked nervously at our own cash flow in the days that followed and found little comfort in his words.

In the 1980's one Peter Clowes of Barlow Clowes fame, had been jailed for 10 years for embezzling £16 million from the financial fund he purported to manage. One particular old lady had invested her savings with his fund, and when the company collapsed, she assumed it was the last she would see of it. However, when she received a compensation cheque for £5000 she decided to send it to us. Andy called that evening with a bunch of flowers, and said he was received by the sweetest old lady you could imagine. He reported her saying; 'I thought I had lost it so when it came back it was a bonus, so I won't miss it if I give it to you.' The Lord does indeed work in marvellous ways.

In view of the success of the 1988 event we felt that we should replicate it during one Christmas weekend in 1990, which we did. But by the spring of 1991 the recession was taking a grip on the economy and, this combined with severe cash flow pressures meant we were forced to place the company into liquidation. In

ANDY HAWTHORNE

You can blame Andy Hawthorne, and his brother Simon, for dreaming up The Message. Together the Hawthorne bros are directors of a Manchester-based fashion and accessory manufacturing company, supplying chain stores like Dorothy Perkins and Top Shop.

Andy has the task of explaining the experience that is The Message at the end of each evening. 'Basically, I'm going to be tying it all together,' he says 'That's if I can keep up with it myself!'

Recognised as a fine communicator to young people, Andy relishes any opportunity to make the truth of Christianity relevant to the vast majority of young people who don't 'do' Church.

1988 saw the launch of The Message and a make over for the two brothers. – Simon choosing the American Baptist pastor look and Andy taking inspiration from Rick Astley.

truth we had concentrated as much on the Message as on the business for around 18 months, and the cash and time investment proved too much.

For those who are not familiar with the system of liquidation I thought I should outline what happens. Effectively, a company who is unable to pay its debts appoints a qualified person or company that looks at the companies affairs and tries to come up with the best outcome for the creditors. It is often the case that the best scenario is that the company owners buy the business back for an agreed amount as once broken up it will often be worthless.

In our case, the appointed liquidator was recommended by our accountant and proved to be a quixotic and imaginative gentleman who, when I informed him that the Inland Revenue had been round to place a charge over our machines exclaimed; 'What did you let them do that for? You should have told them to **** off.' To be honest it was not something I had considered appropriate at the time.

We contacted all of our creditors and apologised about the situation and we were genuine in our offer to pay the debt off, as we wished to re-launch the business. The date of the liquidators meeting, which was not set by us, was bizarrely the first night of the Christmas Message. On the day of the creditors meeting, which we approached with some trepidation, we waited nervously in a meeting room of the Piccadilly Hotel. The meeting was scheduled for 12.00pm and when no one had arrived and at exactly 12.00pm, the liquidator jumped from his chair and said, 'Right were off. If they can't get here on time – tough.'

It was tough for us as well. Not only did we face the uncertainty of the outcome of the liquidation but, as is often the case for Christians, there is the added dimension of trying to find God in a difficult situation. Why would He let that happen when we had believed that the business was to be the platform to launch this ministry?

On the very evening of the day of the liquidators meeting Andy, as event evangelist, had to preach on the goodness of God. Under those circumstances it was a tough call indeed.

CHAPTER 8

EXPANDING THE BUSINESS

We felt that we ought to take a year off from The Message to try and focus on building the business but Mark Pennels, who had been involved in the musical aspects of The Message events, was reluctant to lose the momentum we had gained. He offered to go into schools as 'The Message to Schools,' and asked us to be on a steering group to help support him. We were delighted with this new outcome and Andy was to spend an increasing amount of time with Mark, speaking in assemblies and lunch time concerts. For reasons that I can't recall, Andy thought he could rap, and was soon to join Mark on stage, which would ultimately lead to the formation of The World Wide Message Tribe.

One of our customers at this time was The Western Jean Company, which had been bought out by French Connection. The manager was Gerry Mckenna, an indefatigable and enterprising Scotsman who we worked well with. One day Gerry approached us with the idea of launching our own clothing brand. Over a series of meetings and with the potential of external investment we decided to try our hand at retailing. U-Bahn was launched, initially on Market Street then at alarming speed expanded into 9 new outlets around the country, including the Metro Centre, Gateshead, The Hanley Shopping Centre, and with a £45,000 incentive from the owners, the newly opened Shires shopping mall in Leicester. We also had shops in London, Glasgow and Stoke. But you need very deep pockets to expand at that rate, and when the external investment failed to materialise, we again were forced to close a business.

Whilst Hothouse had remained unaffected by the demise of U-Bahn, the entrepreneurial urge was again satisfied by setting up a 24 hour embroidery business to run parallel with the fashion business, which was now increasingly becoming a wholesaler rather than manufacturer. With an investment of £240,000 into new machinery I believed this was a venture that we needed to make work.

One thing that hadn't changed was the crime rate in Longsight and we began to dread the midnight phone calls from the alarm company. To be woken up at 3.00am and have to drive 16 miles into Manchester to discover damage to the building and missing stock became very wearing. Andy and I would take turns in attending the various break-ins, but when it became increasingly dangerous we would venture out together. Many were false alarms but on one occasion we entered our building to find three lads loading boxes with jackets. We shouted 'Police' and two of them escaped through a window whilst the third must have believed he wouldn't make it and dived behind an embroidery machine. As we went to flush him out he shouted 'I've got a ****ing gun.' I only assumed this wasn't the case when he grabbed a broom and attacked me with it. We managed to subdue him and pinned him down whilst we waited for the police. The alarm had been ripped from the wall and further damage totalling £1,000 was discovered. The case went to court and the young man received £160 fine and a community service order whilst we were left with £1000 worth of uninsured damage and the loss of a quantity of jackets that were never seen again.

The insurance company had by this time insisted we have 24 hour, manned security, but when it was discovered that even the security guards were stealing from us, we despaired. The business was becoming a pressure cooker of unhappiness and it was only a matter of time before Andy felt called to go full time in the schools with Mark, despite the substantial loss of income that he would subsequently experience.

I am sure, in part, that God had put us under pressure to force Andy out of the business, and was willing to allow these difficulties to achieve His purpose. In April 1993 Andy announced that he was to leave and eventually went full time with Mark in the August of that year. The rest of Andy's story can be picked up in his book, 'Diary of a Dangerous Vision,' which tells the story of what has become one of the most dynamic and innovative youth works of our generation, through the drive and dynamism of my brother Andy, of whom I remain enormously proud.

Whilst I totally agreed with, and endorsed his move, it left me with the not inconsiderable problem of managing the business on my own. Andy had been largely responsible for sales for the wholesale business whilst I concentrated on developing the embroidery division – I was not looking forward to handling both on my own. Amazingly and only two weeks after Andy left, I received an unsolicited offer to buy the embroidery business from a customer of ours. I decided to sell up and move the wholesale side with a hand full of key staff to a smaller unit in Whaley Bridge, where I then lived. The quality of life improvement – by no longer having to commute to Manchester – was immediate. I was certainly not going to miss the midnight calls from the alarm company.

Knitted hats were in fashion and providing a steady income in addition to a general upturn in business and we secured a contract with Levis worth £250,000 for their first order alone. It was as if the stopper had come out of the blessings bottle with Andy's decision to leave, and both the business and the Message ministry were beginning to prosper.

Our hats were subcontracted to a company in Hyde, but we were increasingly aware that the Chinese market was attracting substantial volumes of the UK's manufacturing requirements, and when we began to receive new samples faster from Shanghai than up the road in Manchester, I booked a flight to Hong Kong and Shanghai to investigate their potential.

It was like the beginning of the gold rush for the booming Chinese economy and I soon realised that our fortunes were to be made there. We acquired new contracts with Ellesse, Fila, and Adidas as sportswear became more fashionable, and opened an office in Tsuen Wan, on the Kowloon side of Hong Kong in 1996. After spending over £20,000 in one year in the exclusive Harbour Plaza hotel, it made sense to take an apartment and two of our staff moved out to oversee relationships with the factories. My Lexus was soon accompanied by my first Porsche which was soon followed by another and our beautiful farm house in Whaley Bridge completed the picture of a prosperous lifestyle.

In 1997 Hong Kong was handed back to the Chinese after 99 years of Colonial rule. I flew on the last Cathay Pacific aircraft into the old Kai Tak airport, and then in a monumental effort of Chinese efficiency the entire workings were shifted over night to the newly built Chep Lap Kok airport on Lantau island. There was real emotion in the voice of the pilot as we descended onto the tiny strip of tarmac that provided the runway of Kai Tak. It was a genuine hands on experience for the pilot, which I once witnessed from the cockpit of a Jumbo. For the pilot and passengers alike it had remained one of the most exciting airports to land at in the world as you descended between the skyscrapers where you could literally see the inhabitants about their domestic activities. The new airport reflected booming China and Hong Kong reflected the aspirations of the Chinese. It was a place to work hard and make money.

But I was feeling an increasing sense that I wanted to see my business having greater ethical and social purpose and believed that it was my God given duty to find out what that should be. I had remained involved with most of the new initiatives with the Message, but it was never long before my role was replaced and I was called back to business. I also realized that, however large and profitable my business became, however successful I was considered by my peers, in the eternal scheme of things it would be insignificant. The legacy that my life's work would consist of would never be remembered for what I would achieve in business. And yet this was where I was spending most of my time and investing my best efforts.

The exact moment of revelation for me was on the return flight from a sourcing trip in Hong Kong. The Village of Whaley Bridge where I live is on the flight path into Manchester, and as I looked out of the window of the plane, I could see enough details in the landscape below to know it was my home village, as if looking down on a model railway set. Somewhere down there, too small to identify, was my home, family and work place. The fruits of 20 years work were too small to identify. But I suddenly found this revelation liberating as I descended over Stockport, because I realized that my biggest customer, even Adidas – who have their European headquarters there – would hardly be identifiable from this height. Perhaps sometimes it is necessary to get above a situation to gain that new perspective and a realignment of purpose and direction that comes from there.

CHAPTER 9

FINDING THE POOR

The desire to see my business have greater ethical purpose was shortly followed by my first trip to the Third World. I had supported the building of an orphanage in Tanzania that was headed up by my friend Paul Morley who Andy and I had worked with during the Message 88. In 1995, I eventually joined a task force visiting the project as it was nearing completion. There were 21 of us in the working party and by sheer coincidence included Wayne Jeffries, who had been a roadie for The Bill Mason Band.

We flew into Nairobi and then caught several light aircraft with MAF, the Mission Aviation Fellowship – a Christian charity that so excellently serves the needy in remote places across much of Africa. I was disappointed that the Dakota DC3 that we had booked was out of action – due to a broken engine and no spares – as it had always been my favorite plane when I was a boy. I am a committed Christian and a great believer in the power of prayer. All the same, there is something strangely disconcerting about the pilot feeling the need to pray before takeoff. When one of the Cessna's doors blew open in mid flight, the pilot turned to investigate and the plane momentarily nose dived – it suddenly made prayer a very authentic commodity indeed.

Our days at the orphanage were made up of basic laboring and getting to know the locals. I also found myself getting to know God better. It is hard to imagine life now with no mobile phones, internet or e-mail. To be isolated from those, with no method of communication with the outside world was a rarity indeed, towards the end of the 20th century. In the 21st it is almost inconceivable. But when all the 'static' of a Western life style is removed, along with even the good things like your family, the void that is left becomes a place that God can fill with revelation and understanding in a new way.

One of our working party was a young girl named Julie Lancaster. She had seen the project featured on local television in her home town of Clitheroe and had enquired if she could come on the trip. I discovered that her father, John Lancaster, was a businessman having considerable success in double glazing and was Clitheroe's largest employer. Andy and I had been looking to set up a network of Christian businessmen who may support the Message and I enquired if John may come to a fund raising dinner. Though Julie suggested it was unlikely, due to other commitments, John did indeed come to a dinner that took place at the Mottram Hall Hotel in Prestbury, accompanied by his delightful wife, Rose. It was the beginning of a relationship which has blessed and resourced the Message enormously over the years, including two double-decker buses, kitted out for youth work, amazing office and warehouse premises and no shortage of good old Clitheroe cash. It is amazing that such a fortuitous liaison should be birthed in the simplest of villages in the heart of Tanzania, but over the years I hope I have gained some discernment as to what is coincidence and what has the hallmark of divine interaction.

The Tanzanian people inspired in many ways. It was clear that their well developed sense of community and society was integral to their lives, and reflected a value system that is now scarce in the West. Much of their food came from Lake Victoria, on the shores of which both the village and orphanage were situated. The catching of the fish was initiated by two men rowing out in the middle of the night, and dragging a vast net behind them. At first light, what seemed to be every village male, encompassing all ages, met to begin the mighty process of hauling in the catch. As they did so a chant would develop that lasted for the several hours it took to bring the fish in to the shore. Each member of the hauling team sang their part, which ranged from harmonies to solo's, and moved the length of the line in rhythm with the pull of the rope. I was told that the song was also a story that had developed over hundreds of years and was at times rude, at others romantic and of course, being men, often heroic. There was no question that a small diesel engine and pulley could have done the job with one man and in half the time, but a community would be out of work and an exquisite tradition of function and beauty would be lost forever.

Top left – Paul Morley and Simon Hawthorne.
Bottom left – the working party with Julie Lancaster in the red top.

The road from the town of Mwanza to the orphanage was ancient, and continued on to service numerous communities along the length of the lake. Tanzania had won an EEC grant of 30 million

Euros to develop the road and, without the engineering equipment for the task locally, an Italian company had won the contract and vast amounts of machinery had been imported. The pot holed road that had been used for centuries by horse and cart, and latterly by cars and buses, would allow no more that a pedestrian 40 miles per hour, and even that level of promptitude would have been bone shaking.

For generations children had played on, or at the side of the road, and chickens and cattle had wandered its length. The newly applied tarmac meant that drivers discovered their vehicles could now achieve speeds of up to 70 miles an hour, though the road had only been designed to expect a more modest 50. The inevitable consequence was accidents to both human and animal in an unprecedented number. In addition, the excessive speed by heavy wagons soon left the road pot holed in places, and any journey by bus became more akin to a roller coaster at Alton Towers. A short blast at full speed would be followed by a locking of brakes and a violent swerve off a two foot high bank to avoid a chasm in the tarmac and whilst the chassis would follow the inclination of the bank – the body of the vehicle pitched at a far more alarming angle. In true fairground fashion, the screams of the women only encouraged the driver to become more reckless in testing the vehicle's limitations.

The 30 million Euros ran out at some random point along the lake, and the road maintenance, including a significant amount of machinery, was sub-contracted to a group of Indian immigrants, at bargain-basement prices. With no access to spare parts, the machines were cheap enough to plunder and a vast pile of rusting metal soon gathered at the side of the road. Despite the EEC's good intentions apparently little was achieved, other than getting from one place to another more quickly, and what gain is that when there is no measurable improvement to the quality of anyone's life. Unless perhaps those injured by speeding motorists could get to hospital more quickly. Oh no I forgot, they needn't bother as they can't afford the treatment. No, on reflection there really was no benefit to the community at all.

I confess I am not an academic in matters of foreign aid, and feel sure that it is a complex and tortuous to implement, but wouldn't the money have been better spent on ridding the drinking water of bilharzias, a nasty, water born parasite that weakens the body of ten's of thousands and can cause death? Or how many water pumps could be installed for a fraction of that price, so as to irrigate the land for crops, with the vast amounts of fresh water that Lake Victoria could sustainably provide. It is clear that the West has much to give to the developing world, and hoards enough from them to make scathing judgment appropriate. But we too surely have much to learn from them – or perhaps by revisiting our own past, could contemplate the value of a simpler life, and grieve over what we have lost in our own society, in our frantic pursuit of materialism.

Experiencing poverty first hand, I began to understand just why God has such a heart for the poor. I was besotted with these people who lived such uncomplicated lives and managed so well with such meager resources. I was energized by how much good could be done for so very little money, but as the tiny Cessna lifted off from Mwanza airport and banked over Lake Victoria, I wept for the first time in many years, knowing that what I had experienced would not be there to greet me on my home coming. I realised why I also needed to refocus my reason for being in business. I needed to find a purpose in my working life that I had previously failed to achieve. Life is short and very precious so isn't it right that we direct our finances to more than simply acquisitions? Shouldn't we reconsider the words of Jesus who said, 'To whom much is given, much will be required,' and his much ignored command; 'Do not store up for yourselves treasures on earth.'

I took this haunting photograph in Delhi. These beautiful children have been left in an old bath whilst their parents, who are rag pickers go to work. The boredom on their faces tells their story.

CHAPTER 10

THE MISSIONS GRAVEYARD

The Bethany project, as it was named in Mwanza was completed and Paul Morley was arranging a trip to visit an Indian missionary friend he had first met in Uttar Pradesh, whilst he was training a team from Operation Mobilisation, several years earlier. Paul invited me along and I was keen to join him.

On a previous visit, Paul had written to his friend, Daniel Inbaraj, who had recently married, to say that he wished to visit him and stay for six weeks, and requesting he meet him at the airport. The letter was never received, and when Paul arrived at Delhi airport he had to negotiate his way to Orai by several trains on his own. He eventually arrived in the early hours of the morning and managed to find the Daniels home. After knocking for some time on the door, Daniel eventually answered and, to his astonishment discovered a white man stood there, complete with suitcase.

The following morning Selvi prepared a modest breakfast of egg and bread for Paul and he enquired why they weren't eating with him. Selvi appeared sheepish as she explained that she wasn't hungry but Paul guessed that this may be all the food they had in the house. It transpired that they had literally no money left and that morning Selvi had decided to sell her gold necklace that was given as a dowry gift at the time of her wedding. Paul's timing, or perhaps God's, was perfect, and though not a wealthy man, he had enough money to stay with them for six weeks and help restructure their lives and finances.

Uttar Pradesh has a population of over 190 million and is India's most populace state. It is the same size as Great Britain where we often feel over crowded so spare a thought for U.P. as it is also known. Uttar Pradesh has an important place in the culture of India; it is considered to be the birthplace of Hinduism, has been the ancient seat of Hindu religion, learning and culture, and has many important sites of Hindu pilgrimage. For this reason U.P. has remained a tough nut to crack for the many Christian mission organisations that have tried.

U.P. remains one of India's more backward states where the female literacy rate is dismal at 43%. However, the male literacy situation is reasonably better at 70%. It remains the case though that the proportion of Dalit women can number as low as 2% literacy in many rural villages.

Paul Morley invited me to join him on his next trip to India and I was keen to accept as it was a country I have always held a fascination for. Indeed my Great Grandfather, an Irishman named Robert Hawthorne, had been on the first missionary expedition to India with the Salvation Army in 1883, accompanying William Booth's nephew. We believe he arrived in Bombay complete with Salvation Army uniform, but quickly realised that they would be too easily confused with the occupying British Army, and that developing trusting relationships would be very difficult to achieve unless they were to adopt the local dress. Phil Wall, at the time he was National Youth Leader for the Salvation Army, managed to access the library at their head office in London and photocopy a record of the mission trip. Robert records his joy at walking barefoot for miles, in harmony with the natives and his surroundings.

So perhaps India was in my blood. I recall one of my close friend's, saying at the time of my conversion that; 'It was always on the cards.' I regret not investigating why he felt that was the case but there must have been something that had drawn him to that conclusion. I was certainly no saint. I don't believe 'the cards' can predict anything, but when I arrived in India for the first time it certainly seemed to be with a sense of what some would call fate drawing me there, though I prefer to believe it was a sense of God's leading.

We flew into Delhi and caught a train for the five hour journey to Jhansi, where Daniel Inbaraj met us with his wife Selvi, before travelling on by jeep for a further three hour journey. It is customary in India for a family to adopt the Christian name of the father as the Sir-name – hence they would be referred to collectively as 'the Daniels.' They had moved to Uttar Pradesh from the more affluent and pleasant Madras or Chennai as it is now known, after qualifying with English Degrees.

Orai is one of the dustiest places I have ever visited, and even a short jeep ride will leave a thin layer of filth over you and your possessions. It is probably also the mosquito capital of the world, where they gather in their evil multitudes. I recall spotting a large, dark cloud and commenting to Daniel that it looked like it may rain, which seemed unlikely as it was their dry season. Daniel corrected me by pointing out it was mosquitoes, probably in their billions. A visit to the Daniels' toilet is only to be ventured after applying a significant amount of insect repellent and never at night, and only the most diligent attention to the placing of your mosquito net will save you from a night of misery.

The climate is pleasant for the months of November or March, otherwise it is cold for three months, hotter than the sun for five and hotter than the sun and wetter than the Indian Ocean for the other four.

Following one particularly hot trip, where everyone in our party was ill with some particularly nasty strain of Orai dysentery, we had to confess that we Brits are not as tough as we would like to believe, and determined that we would limit ourselves to visiting in early spring or late autumn. Therefore if we did get ill, we wouldn't bake in our own vomit at the same time.

On one particular occasion I had fallen ill and was feeling like death when I had to catch the school bus to Jhansi, or risk missing the train, and ultimately our flight home. I was seriously beginning to pray that God would take me heavenwards early, and spare me the three hour journey of pot holed roads and baking heat that awaited us.

The temperature inside the bus was like a sauna, but to open the windows meant that the air, which was even hotter outside, could cause you to pass out. We stopped wherever we saw someone selling refrigerated drinks, but within five minutes it was like drinking from the hot tap. It was at this time that Daniel turned to me and said 'Why did you not get the train, that would be better isn't it?' It transpired that there was a perfectly efficient, cheap and air-conditioned train that ran regularly from Orai to Jhansi, but which Daniel had failed to mention. My knuckles gradually became white as I considered throttling him, but realized I no longer had the strength.

'Delhi belly,' as you will have gathered is not limited to Delhi. Indeed, I would rate Orai as the number one place on earth that you are most likely to get ill. Having said that, Delhi has not been lax in trying to regain the crown and did me in mightily one year when mysteriously, my colleagues emerged unscathed. When I was well enough to speak, we compared notes as to what I may have eaten that the others had not, and concluded that the only thing it could have been was pickled onions. This seems unlikely I know, but I have seen one tea spoon full of Indian pickles poleax gangs of strong men, so fellow travelers be warned.

Following a meal in a safe-looking restaurant, we had been sitting in Connaught Place, which is a large park in the centre of Delhi, where the locals can find a rare, open space to chat and perhaps buy an ice cream. These come in various flavors, including dysentery and cholera flavor, so we have learned to avoid them, but the locals still seem keen.

Paul had suffered from an ear infection, possibly from the manky water that we had baptized some delightful new believers in, during our trip to Gannavaram. We were relaxing and enjoying a snake charmer waving a flute at a gently swaying and hypnotised Cobra, when a man grabbed Paul's ear lobe and immediately diagnosed a blockage. How he knew to select Paul I have no idea, but before he could protest the man produced a loop of wire and began extracting great balls of wax from the offending ear, and wiping it on the back of his hands. 'It is hearing better yes?' he kept saying, and Paul had no reason other than to agree with him. Indeed he suddenly noticed the birds were singing and happily handed over 30 Rupees for the man's services. I on the other hand was beginning to feel unwell and decided to return to the hotel, by which time I was feeling alarmingly chilly, despite the temperature being a pleasant 27 degrees. I climbed into a sleeping bag and covered myself with blankets, then even more blankets but still felt cold as my stomach contents turned to a gurgling mass of evil. After three hours of throwing up until only my colon was still in place, and even that seemed ready to dislodge, and the other end began to pass more water than a Mumbai monsoon, I eventually burst the blood vessels in my eyes from the pressure of throwing up and developed a prolific nose bleed. Had I possessed a revolver I would have shot myself but instead began to produce enough wind to run a small turbine. Only the fearsome rumours of infected needles stopped me phoning for an ambulance. After a miserable night spent naked in the bath, by the morning it had begun to pass – though my bright red eyes caused me to resemble Beelzebub for several weeks afterwards. 'Too much information,' I hear you say. On the contrary, I spared you most of it.

But if I were a gambling man I would back Orai for the worst bacterial infestations any day. Disinfectant has yet to be imported, and the open sewers are the home to most of the world's worst pathogens.

I have long held a theory that, when Satan was kicked out of heaven he set up camp in Orai and to pass the time, started a mosquito factory, which is still in full production today. So I have the greatest respect for Daniel and Selvi, who suffer all this and

more for the sake of the Gospel and for the children who learn, not just an education, but a Christian value system that equips them for life as equals in an unequal world.

The Daniels had begun a small school, initially in their home, and at the time we visited, had expanded into a disused warehouse, without windows and with a dirt floor. That said, the children were happy and clearly receiving a good education.

Initially, the Daniels had suffered considerable hostility as Christians and when they refused to have a Hindu God displayed in their window during a festival, were almost lynched by a mob of fanatics. Daniel was forced to stay indoors for three months until the death threats subsided. When they opened the school, they named it Mizpeh, taken from the Old Testament and meaning watchtower. The addition of 'Christian School' to the signage had again caused death threats, but they had persisted and today the sign is still clearly displayed outside the school building.

Daniel and Selvi's home was next door to the local wedding hall and November is traditionally the wedding season. November is also a good time to visit India as the weather is pleasantly warm and the monsoon has passed. Summer is out of the question, when the humidity is suffocating and temperatures can soar to a very unpleasant 49 degrees. Power cuts are still common throughout rural India, where 40 million people still do not have electricity, so an electric fan or air conditioning is mere fantasy, and probably not affordable in any case.

The wedding hall was owned by a middle-aged man who we came to understand had wished to acquire the land to build his hall, but when the owner declined his offer – he shot him. The case went to court but he was sufficiently wealthy enough to bribe the judge and the case was dismissed.

Most weddings are arranged by the parents of the bride and groom, and it is sometimes the case that the couple may not even meet until their wedding day. Our Western desire for independence at the earliest opportunity leads us to believe that arranged marriages are an oppressive system that has no place in modern society, and whilst there are many tales in the British press of abusive Asian parents enforcing marriage for their own convenience or against their children's wishes, at their best - arranged marriages are a practice that results in strong family commitment and a remarkably low divorce rate.

The ceremony would often begin after we had gone to bed, and would be announced by a group of around 30 men on the Asian equivalent of a stag night. They gathered inside a rectangle of fluorescent lights, held vertically and linked by an electric cable. The lights were powered by a generator – as was the PA system: both were onboard a human-powered, wooden cart. The PA system and giant speaker, blasted out Indian music at an ear-splitting volume. It is the tradition in India, to turn the volume up to the maximum level until it distorts, possibly in this case to drown out the din of the generator, and add as much reverb as available.

The assembly of the groom's friend's start at one end of town – once they have taken sufficient liquor – and then they dance their way down the high street, making sleep impossible for anyone along the route. Indians seem remarkably tolerant of other people's noise and will accept festivals, fireworks and car horns at a level that would make the Noise Abatement Society in our country more than a little choleric.

On our first experience of the preliminary celebrations of an Indian wedding, we ran out excitedly and were enthusiastically invited to join in the celebrations. On this particular trip we had taken two girls with us who were part of Paul Morley's 'Task Force,' that worked in schools in Scunthorpe. The girls, quite innocently joined in the dancing, much to the delight of the men. The following day, the Daniels were subject to an endless list of complaints from neighbors accusing them of entertaining the equivalent of prostitutes. We had clearly committed a faux pas of some magnitude.

The groom eventually arrived astride a lavishly decorated white horse, and wearing a bejeweled turban. A period of peace would follow, as the guests entered the hall for the marriage dedications. However sleep would be short lived as three hours of fireworks, mainly what we would know as air bombs, would follow. As the first bang went off I recall Paul muttered from his bed, 'He's lifted the veil, took one look at his new wife – decided against and shot her.'

Much of India has retained an unfortunate deference to Westerners, which may be partly due to caste inequality indoctrinating a sense of unworthiness, or perhaps a legacy from the days of the Raj. Indians are also remarkably sociable and in either case we were always a great novelty when visiting the town and would quickly gather a crowd of people wishing to practice their English. In Orai we have had to avoid spending too much time lingering on the high street, as the crowd can soon stop the traffic and attract the attention of the stick-wielding police, which they will use indiscriminately to disperse such a gathering.

English is the business language of India, and this is never lost on Government officials and the police who wish to give their children the best education available. It soon became apparent to them that this was being offered by the Daniels and with the patronage of local politicians, who also began to enroll their children; the Daniels gained some protection from the militant Hindus. Amazingly, in this Hindu stronghold, the children attending Mizpeh school were receiving the best Christian education that I have ever experienced, in any country I have visited.

Uttar Pradesh is known as 'The Mission's Graveyard' due to the historic, spectacular failure of Christian mission in the state. Here in Orai, despite opposition and considerable hardship, the Daniels had managed to establish a Christian school and church and it seemed to me that we needed to support them. Having purchased eight acres of land we began to invest into the infrastructure and soon had a substantial building that could educate around 450 children, with living accommodation for the Daniels and around 80 boarding children.

Mizpeh is a fee paying school, but even though the fees are very modest it remains the case that many parents cannot afford to pay for their children and so there are around 40 sponsored places for the very poor. Each year, around 450 children receive an excellent education and almost all go onto further education at University. In addition, many hear the Gospel message in a way that would not be possible without the school and many make decisions for Christ, despite opposition from their parents. A church meets every Sunday on the school grounds and about 40 believers attend. I believe it remains as the only evangelical witness to a city of half a million people and a pilot light of faith that must not be extinguished and become yet another headstone in the mission's graveyard. The Daniels believed their call to Orai was as evangelists, but realized that they could achieve so much more for the people by meeting educational and spiritual needs together.

Our first school opened in Orai, Uttar Pradesh and is managed by Pastor Daniel Inbaraj and his wife Selvi. Currently 450 children attend with most going on to further studies at College or University.

In the early years of visiting them we bought push bikes and travelled into outlying villages where motorised vehicles could not gain access. The people were invariably friendly and generous in their hospitality and would listen with interest to our stories, but with 30 million gods in Hinduism it is difficult for Jesus to not become just another. It is also very common to see an image of Jesus alongside Ganesh, the elephant god, or Shiva, the destroyer. In India, it is true, and understandable that you will try to take all the help you can get from wherever you can get it.

In our early days and before the advent of mobile phones and e-mail we were isolated from contacting home unless we could find an STD shop where the telephone lines were working. In some of the villages we visited, we were honored as the first white people to visit – incredible when you consider Britain ruled India for several hundred years. But few people ever visited these rural areas and still don't. Indeed, Queen Victoria never visited India though it was the most populace part of her empire. In the 18 years we have been visiting Orai we have never seen another white face. But that still remains true of much of India, and perhaps inevitable in view of its enormous size.

The Daniels have three boys, Jachin, Theo and Boaz. All have achieved Masters Degrees, having been educated at good schools in Chennai. Degrees are becoming so common in India that it will often take at least a high caliber Masters to be considered for the best jobs. The boy's commitment to their parents is unquestioned and they all contribute financially or practically to the work in the schools as is expected within their custom. It has been our privilege to watch them grow up over the years to be fine young men and to now see them coming under concerted pressure from Selvi to choose one of the many wives that she consistently puts forward for them. I met Boaz recently and was surprised to see he had cut his hair short in contrast to the shoulder length, Western style he has carried for several years. He explained that a potential bride had been sought for his brother Jachin, and that it was expected of him to be smart and tidy when the prospective mother-in-law visited, a sacrifice that would be a rarity indeed in Britain.

Though palm leaf houses are slowly being replaced by brick ones they remain a common sight in northern India

In November 2010 I received an e-mail from Selvi saying that they had a new son. Not this time by birth but from a newly born child that had been dumped outside the school in a plastic bag. The baby was discovered by a lorry driver relieving himself in a ditch. The umbilical was still intact and ants were biting the baby when it was handed over to the school's night watchman. The Daniels cleaned the baby and had him checked over in hospital. They felt the child had been sent to them and so applied for adoption. The baby has suitably been named, Moses. Not Moses in the basket, this is a contemporary story of Moses in the plastic bag. It will probably never be discovered who the baby's mother was. Perhaps the child was illegitimate and the mother had been able to conceal this from her husband. The consequence for her could have been death. Or perhaps the child was just one too many mouths for that family to feed.

Many of the villages we visited offered near biblical scenes of simplicity, where women still gathered water from the communal well, and goats and cows grazed from the mountain of hay in the yard. Other women, in brightly coloured saris, cooked at wooden stoves or ground spices in hand-carved, stone bowls, whilst the men worked the field before returning in the evening to their homes of thatched roof and mud walls. The ubiquitous buffalo is the animal of choice for those who can afford one. Though large, it is docile and provides around 20 litres of milk per day for the family. Their extraordinary, swinging gait is unforgettable and reminiscent of a creature from Star Wars, as they head to a watering hole after a hard days labour, often supervised by a small boy with a stick and providing a quintessentially-Indian scene. The work horse of the fields is the oxen which can carry or pull great weight or be used to plough the fields. It is a community where nothing goes to waste nor can they afford it to. It is common to see a woman, elegant in her sari yet carrying a basket of buffalo dung in a basket on her head. The dung will be formed into semi circles and when dried – stacked into neat domes to be later used as fuel during the winter months.

Accompanying this apparently idyllic, rural life, is toil and poverty where a farmer may expect to earn no more than .75p per day. Medical bills can often be beyond the reach of many village people, who also cannot afford the fees to educate their children who instead work the fields, often before they are even teenagers, adding to the 50 million child-labourers in India today.

For girls, life can be particularly cruel as they are considered a liability to many families and often sold to meet a medical need or pay a debt. Once sold, they will be subject to long hours of monotonous, hard work and until the debt is repaid, will remain under ownership of their master. Due to the extortionate rates of interest charged, they may never gain their freedom. It is estimated that as many as 15 million children are in bonded labour in India today. Girls are particularly vulnerable to being trafficked from there into the sex trade, which numbers 1.2 million under-age girls out of the estimated 3 million prostitutes in India. Most are Dalits. Once trapped, their lives are miserable and they will often be expected to have sex with as many as 20 men or more in one day, in return for little more than food or a sound beating for refusal. The Police, the 7th most corrupt force in the world, will often turn a blind eye to the child sex trade, many of those being on the pay roll of the brothels and given free access to its women.

Mumbai is considered to be one of the major sex trafficking destinations for victims of commercial sex exploitation in the world today. There is evidence that 10% of the Police force of Mumbai have AIDS, 5 times the national average, as a result of sleeping with prostitutes, often through payment in lieu of turning a blind eye to illegal brothels.

The cruelest certitude is that the Dalit is untouchable until it comes to sex. This appalling duplicity, as a direct result of the caste system, must surely rank as an outrage against humanity, and confirm that these trafficked women and children deserve a voice and an advocate that will bring their perpetrators to justice.

Each year in India, thousands of girls are dedicated to a temple goddess in a ceremony that begins a lifetime of prostitution. In a wedding ceremony where no groom will come to meet them, instead they are wed – dedicated to a temple goddess and their lives will be spent as a devadasi or temple prostitute.

A string of red and white beads strung on saffron coloured thread is worn around the necks of the devadasi.

A few are paid, others receive only food and are expected to stay close to the temple to sleep with priests or other men their parents have struck an agreement with. Some return to their homes to be auctioned off as mistresses for as long as men will have them. Most of them wind up in the brothels of india's major cities.

Despite India's government passing laws forbidding the practice of temple prostitution, the centuries old religious tradition continues for 100,000s of thousands of its women.

Organisations like International Justice Mission, (IJM) and the Dalit Freedom network, (DFN) and dare I say ourselves through the work of Life Association, are working hard to raise awareness and end the vile practice of child prostitution, but there is much still to do.

Through the Indian national census of 2011, the current demographic of age and gender can be calculated and it appears there are approximately 52 million girls between the age of 12 – when it is considered they may enter puberty, and 16 when they would no longer be considered children. The India Government's own figure of 1.2 million child prostitutes is taken from this figure, though Save The Children claim it is probably much higher. A simple calculation reveals that there must therefore be 1 in 43 of the girls in India in prostitution – to the shame of the nation.

While girls are often trafficked from neighboring countries such as Bangladesh and Nepal, the vast majority are Indian nationals from the Dalit community, hailing from northern, northeastern and central India. These regions are home to various communities like the Kanjars, Nats, Bedias, Rajnats and Bachadas where prostitution is an expectation of females as a means of financial provision for the family. Hence children coming from these sub castes are often sold by their own families into a miserable life of abuse. With such indoctrination and low self esteem, it is inevitable that some girls and women, even when rescued find it is only too easy to return to the misery of prostitution when bills need to be paid.

The United Nations estimates that there are 27 million people who have been trafficked in the world today, into some form of modern day slavery. That is five times more than the number of people in slavery when William Wilberforce forced through an act of Parliament banning slavery 200 years ago. Of these 27 million, over half live in India, making India the world centre for people trafficking. Most of these slaves are Dalits.

According to the U.K. Home Office there are at most 8000 people trafficked in the UK – being 0.3% of the UN figure and around 800,000 in Europe making up just 3%. India alone will have over 15 million trafficked individuals. This does not include the 50 million that are in bonded labour in that country, which is modern day slavery by any measure.

CHAPTER 11

GANNAVARAM

Over the years we have had many requests for help or financial assistance and discerning which are valid is always difficult. In the spring of 1993, Paul Morley received a letter from a young Indian man named Paul Raju. He had read an article written by Paul Morley, which appeared in a Christian magazine in the UK – though we have no idea how it ended up in a small village called Gannavaram, in Andhra Pradesh. He was a pastor's son, and was attempting to raise money for a push bike to enable him to help orphans in outlying villages. We were curious to meet him and so Paul wrote to him, asking if he would be interested in meeting us in Orai. He agreed, and traveled with two companions on the 30 hour train journey to the Daniels home.

Andhra Pradesh, also called A.P, is known as the rice bowl of India which makes up 77% of its total crop. It also produces large amounts of cotton which is an industry that employs 450,000 children nationally – 250,000 in A.P. alone. It has been estimated that as few as 5% of girls under the age of 14 still live in some of the rural villages in India, most having been sold to work as bonded labourers. These unfortunate girls in A.P. are mostly employed in the cotton fields where their small fingers and compliant spirits are harnessed to pollinate the cotton seeds for remarkably low wages and sometimes for only food.

I had first hand experience of this when I launched my clothing brand Ascension and visited the cotton fields and our Fairtrade supply chain. The Fairtrade foundation works primarily for the farmer/grower groups and monitors the whole supply chain through to the finished product. Despite having Fairtrade accreditation the cotton producers were still employing children prior to the farmer harvesting the crop and there were no early signs of this practice being addressed. I remain a supporter of Fairtrade products, who by their own admission are not perfect but remain amongst the best and most widely supported supplier of fair-trade products. It remains the case that even with their best efforts, the supply chain of the garment industry will often have unfairness woven somewhere within it.

With the exception of several fairly lengthy delays, we have had, in the main, positive experiences on our numerous train journeys across India. Most of these delays may be forgiven, in view of the complexity of the vast, Indian rail-network. Sadly, for nostalgia's sake, steam has given way to diesel and electric trains, and travelling on the roof is discouraged. This is a shame as I had always wanted to experience journeying that way, though I imagine tunnels might have been challenging. Indian railways are one of the world's largest employers, with 1.6 million employees on hand to ensure these monolithic conveyancers deliver the nations millions around the country at remarkably affordable prices, from a Westerner's point of view at least.

Most trains offer 3 tier (meaning three beds layered on top of each other), which is the cheapest carriage – apart from open wooden seating – then 3 tier or 2 tier with AC, and occasionally 1st AC, which is a carriage with just three single compartments. Even then, when I have treated my wife and I to this luxury, the price for a 20 hour journey is only around £30.

20 hour train journeys may sound like a drag, but with a comfortable bunk, a book and some music, the time soon passes.

They have yet to ban hanging out of the doorways, and as the scenic splendor of the Indian countryside passes by, it is a welcome break from the frantic pace of life that is usually our lot in the 21st century.

Trains seem to reflect much of Indian society's ambivalence to litter. At the major train stations, a small army of men will board the train with boiler suits back sprays of disinfectant – making them look like a scene from the film Ghost Busters. They deal with the toilets but the passengers' habit of putting the litter from the many meals served on a lengthy journey onto the floor of the aisles makes the train a tip.

The toilets are open to the railway lines and, where as this is not a problem in the countryside, it makes the stations pretty disgusting. Rats are abundant and seem to be largely tolerated whilst a meager living is gleaned from rag picking along the station track by those unfortunate enough to have made their living there.

Our many train journeys have been comfortable enough but the same luxuries are not always there for the poor, and Paul Raju's modest salary of .50p per week had ensured he was travelling in the train equivalent of steerage class. The train was also packed, and his colleagues and he had to stand for much of the journey. He stayed with us for a few days and we judged him to be a genuine, if shy young man, and readily paid for his train journey and the push bike he wanted.

We received a photograph of the new bike about a month later and an accompanying letter describing the 40 miles he was travelling each day to take food and medicines to the orphans. In addition, he had a plan to buy a piece of land and build an orphanage, 'God willing,' which over the years we have come to understand usually means; if the white man is willing. We determined to visit him on our next trip, and in March of the following year flew to Madras where Paul greeted us with a large

Paul Raju with the original bicycle we bought him that has covered many hundreds of miles around the local villages.

banner declaring, 'welcome Reverend Paul Morley and Reverend Simon Hawthorne.' Titles are issued freely in India and I was more recently elevated to; The Reverend, Doctor, Simon Hawthorne for services to the community in Andhra Pradesh. I am also regularly referred to as 'Spicy Simon,' which I feel is far more appropriate.

Paul Raju had hired a mini bus to travel the 400 kilometers to Gannavaram. As we loaded our bags into the vehicles, I asked him how long the journey would take. 'Oh, surely no more than 5 hours,' he assured me. After six hours I was feeling sick due to tarmac being only a rumour on most sections of the road and, on reflection an ill-advised samosa I had purchased at the airport. After throwing up out of the window I again enquired how much further it would be, and Paul assured me that we would; 'surely be there in an hour or two.' I continued to embellish the left hand side of the mini bus with the entire contents of my stomach and eventually, and with a total journey time of 14 hours, we arrived. Having travelled the same journey, admittedly in the opposite direction, but in the same vehicle and on the same road, you may wonder why he could be so inaccurate in his estimation. Except that he wasn't. He was telling me what I wanted to hear. This is common within the culture of Indians, whether Christian or not, and can easily lead to frustration, and may even seem deceitful, until you understand this anomaly better. When trying to explain this phenomena to someone who has experienced it for the first time, I compared it to my wife, spending ages getting ready to go out for the evening, then coming downstairs wearing my least favorite dress. 'How do I look?' she asks. 'Really nice darling, you look great,' you lie through your teeth. It is telling her what she wants to hear, so as not to disappoint her.

This highly developed habit of Indians causes particular problems in commerce. My business manager in Mumbai, Solomon, is one of the most delightful, honest and spiritual people I know. However, he flatly refuses to inform me of bad news, e.g. delayed deliveries, damaged goods, or monsoon damaged stock, because this is bad news. Delivery dates are always given with excessive optimism. 'The goods will surely be ready in three weeks.' This assumes that there will be no strikes, which are common, religious festivals, which seem to take place every other week, and a plethora of other things that will ensure that date would only have been achieved if all 30 million Indian gods were real, and turned up with their mates to lend a hand.

Indians also operate on something that I refer to as; 'Indian time.' The same principle of unrealistic optimism applies, but in general terms, the Indian culture means that time is a very flexible commodity indeed. 'At 9.00am,' means 11.00am. 'Tomorrow,' means next week and 'soon.' means a very, very long wait, and so on.

Having inspected the land that Paul Raju wished to buy and having investigated his costings, we agreed to send him the money to buy 2 acres of land and to erect a small building of brick walls and thatched roof. We were pleased to see he had completed the work on time when we visited him some six months later, and held a church service to celebrate the opening. A number of local pastors had come to join us, some wondering if further buildings were to be forthcoming in their direction, and some who genuinely seemed to want to be a part of celebrating this new work.

An elderly couple joined us for the service and, through an interpreter, told us their amazing story. They were both committed Hindus with no knowledge of Christianity. The man was retired and spent much of his time gathering wood for the fire for cooking. One day, whilst splitting a log with a machete, he mistimed his stroke and impaled the blade in his foot. With no local doctor or access to medicine, the wound soon became infected and eventually gangrenous, and the man was very close to death. One night, as he lay on his bed he had a dream where Jesus appeared to him, by name, and told him he was going to be well and that he must visit the church. He woke in the morning and indeed his foot was much improved so he found his wife to tell her of his dream. To his astonishment she had had exactly the same dream, and both agreed they must enquire where a church of Jesus may be found and so had eventually come to the new, thatched building, which Paul Raju had erected. The foot was completely healed.

Both India and Africa are abundant in such stories where they often appear common place. In contrast, they seem comparatively rare in the West and I have often wondered why this is. Certainly in Africa, the voodoo culture makes awareness of the supernatural far more prevalent so perhaps more dramatic manifestations of good and evil are experienced. In the West, our more cynical and scientific approach may mean that similar events are squashed before they have a chance to manifest themselves. Whether this is the case or not, and for whatever reason, my own experience has been that I have experienced a greater sense of God's presence, and His input, when I have been in the Developing World. One such example was when I was to preach at a church service in a small and very rural village in Africa. We had been invited by a local pastor who didn't speak English and through a translator had received directions to his church. We arrived in good time to the sound of African women singing. Their amazing voices and deep, rich harmony reverberated around the room as they swayed to the rhythm of their song. It soon became apparent that no one spoke English and I was at a loss to know how my talk was going to be understood. I considered busking it 'in tongues' and hoping for the best but it soon became clear that the pastor had come to the same conclusion and that an interpreter was needed.

He disappeared as my team and I made a pitiful attempt at singing an English chorus and about 15 minutes later, reappeared with a smart young man in a suit and tie, who introduced himself with near perfect English. It transpired that the young man was studying at a bible college in a large town many miles away and was on route to visit a church in another village. He had caught the bus but got off at the wrong stop when he was spotted by the pastor who he had never met. On hearing the pastor's predicament, the young man judged our need was greater and agreed to join us. Not only was he a great translator but, I believe, a divine provision. Of course coincidences do happen. It would be a strange thing in such a complex world if they did not, but 30 years of experience of walking with God, has I believe, given me some discernment to allow me to differentiate between a chance happening and when His interaction with me is taking place.

There is a popular phrase in evangelical circles; 'miracles don't produce faith – faith produces miracles.' This suggests that the miraculous acts of God are initiated by us through our faith. I have heard of God described as being shy – who without invitation seems reluctant to act or intervene – like someone hiding badly behind a bush but really wanting to be discovered – if you would forgive such irreverence. I think this attribute of shyness, is probably true, though of course the English language does not convey the meaning properly in the word 'shy.' It seems strange to have the creator of all things described this way, but I have come to recognise that this may be a strange attribute of God – Almighty, omnipotent and shy? There were certainly times when Jesus appeared so, urging those healed by him to remain silent – appearing and interacting more often to the humble, or those genuinely seeking, and most of all those who recognised their need. 'Without faith, it is impossible to please God.' says Hebrews 11. Perhaps therefore it is no wonder that He does not appear to those who choose not to believe. If we are to come to him as Jesus suggests 'as little children' as recorded in Matthew 18 v 3 – 'I tell you the truth, unless you change and become like little children, you will never enter the kingdom of heaven,' then arrogance and pride are attributes that would presumably distance us from him and are also not normally associated with children.

Paul Raju proved a good steward and we were keen to develop the project and over a period of several years, built a substantial, three-story building to be used as a school and home for 150 children. Gannavaran is situated about 45 minutes east of Vijayawada, the main town in the area with a population of 2.2 million. In contrast Gannavaram is a delightfully peaceful village, accessed by a series of winding tracks through fields of cotton and rice, and ringed by palm trees. Most of the population is employed in agriculture, returning from their fields only as light fades. Oxen drag ploughs across fields as they have for centuries and Buffalo wallow in muddy pools by the road side as women return from the well with large, clay water bowls on their heads.

Village girls preparing delicious coconut chutney –
a popular south Indian breakfast and served with idli.

All the years we had known him, Paul Raju had sported a generous beard, in contrast to the ubiquitous moustache preferred by most Indian men. We often teased him about it, saying that he would never find a wife as it would tickle her too much. We assumed we must have taken this too far when one day we received a letter informing us that he had shaved and his father had found a wife for him. In view of the haste of the wedding we were unable to attend but a few weeks later received a photo of a clean shaven Paul with very miserable looking wife. In fact he didn't look too happy himself. It was with some trepidation that we eventually returned to Gannavaram but were relieved to find his new wife Krupa to be delightful, with the most wonderful smile and no small amount of skill in the kitchen. For reasons that are not apparent, smiling for a photo, even on your wedding day, is not customary in India.

It was not long before Krupa was pregnant and gave birth to a son, and in keeping with the multiplication rate in India, wasted no time in getting pregnant again. However, after several months she miscarried, and grieved the loss of her baby. Several weeks later a mid wife called at the children's home with a baby girl that had been dumped at the doorway of the hospital. Paul informed the midwife that they only received children aged four and above but Krupa insisted she see the baby and immediately fell in love with her. After several days of persistence, Paul relented and they adopted the baby and appropriately named her Grace.

All of the children at the school come from the poorest backgrounds and are brought to us by grandparents or neighbours, after the children's parents have died or have no longer been able to look after them. It is heartbreaking but inevitable that some are turned away simply through a lack of resources. It is often the case that a widow will come, and in desperation ask us to take her child or children from her. Women are very dependent on their husbands to provide for them and often struggle to find paid work and suffer abuse following the death of a husband. In such cases the brother or father-in-law will often claim the property of the widow and if they have no fondness for her, simply kick her out with nothing. Though illegal, this practice remains commonplace. Where possible, we will take the mother in as well as there is always a need for hard working cooks and cleaners in such a busy place as a children's home.

The day begins early, accompanied by the crowing of cockerels and the barking of dogs claiming territory, and soon the chatter of children going about early morning washing and various other chores can be heard. After a hearty breakfast of rice and spicy vegetables, lessons begin and will continue through the day with an hours break for lunch.

A teacher in a rural village may expect to earn no more than £1000 a year and most prefer a better paid job in the city. Still

Our school and children's home in Gannavaram and some of the children celebrating Republic Day.

many of the children at the Life Association school have excelled and gone on to further education. Above all else they are safe from abuse, or being trafficked to swell the scandalous number of working children in India, and they are loved and valued and that must count for something in this vast country where people so often appear to be no more than a disposable commodity.

Each year, around Easter time we have held a pastors' conference to provide some encouragement and teaching for these men who lead isolated and difficult lives. The numbers have grown to around 150 plus wives and we are only too aware that some are coming more for the edible food than the spiritual kind. But many are genuine folk who have committed themselves to serve the people of a particular village in any way they can, and having no qualifications or training are keen to learn from us.

Some of the pastor's who we have ordained into ministry in Andhra Pradesh.

A consequence of a lack of a formal education is harassment from the Police, often looking for a back-hander. So we took the initiative of ordaining many of them and providing an official looking ordination certificate, readily available from Microsoft Word. Being written in English and with an authentic looking stamp, it apparently worked wonders when waved in front of the Police.

One such young man from Macilipatnam particularly caught our attention. His name was Jae Ru, and we learned that he lived in a slum colony on the coast, on a meager strip of land donated by the Government, to the Dalit community. Amongst them were lepers in various stages of physical decay. This is a disgrace, as the World Health Organisation has committed to providing free medicine across the globe to eradicate the disease, but apathy has meant that the drugs are not distributed or else sold on by corrupt officials.

We travelled the two and a half hour journey to the colony, to discover a community of around 140 families. Their homes were a mix of thatched palm leaf walls and roofs combined with plastic sheeting, and averaging no more that 3 sq meters in diameter. The conditions for these people would be difficult in the dry season, but in the monsoon, without raised floors and sealed roofs, would be unimaginable.

The Government had designated a strip of land alongside a railway line and put one water tap in to service the community. The supply came on for just half an hour a day, and to miss your turn meant a long wait before the precious water came again.

The families survived by a combination of rag picking and recycling rubbish and the children were employed as rat pickers – catching vermin at the railway station for which they were paid a pittance. There was no access to education, and the people were simply left to their own devices, to live or die, it didn't seem to matter to the authorities. I fell in love with them.

Our new school opened in the slum village in Machilipatnam in 2011.

Machilipatnam is a large town on the coast of Andhra Pradesh in the middle of the cut out of the east side of India, about half way down in the Bay of Bengal. Like much of the South East coast of India, Machilipatnam had been badly affected by the Tsunami on Boxing Day 2004, where the sea had come inland, up to three miles in places. The home of Pastor Yakub, whom we knew from our pastors' conferences, had been badly damaged and many fishermen and their families had lost their lives. We were keen to help with any aid we could raise, and took clothes and what money we could, but it felt pitifully inadequate in the face of such devastated lives. But there was something we could do for the leper colony that had no education. We could build a school and in the spring of 2011, with a celebration of dignitaries, a government minister and 500 locals we opened our new school for the slum children. Who knows what great things these children will achieve with their lives now they have the opportunity through education?

A days labour for 30 men produces only a modest
catch of fish for themselves and their families.

CHAPTER 12

MUMBAI

Mumbai is home to 17 million people and generates 38% of the tax revenues of India. It is the financial center of the country and of course, home to the film industry known as Bollywood. It boasts more Billionaires than London and, amazingly, has some of the most expensive real estate in the world. It is actually surrounded by water and, like Hong Kong and Manhattan, has not allowed its isolation to deter it from becoming a major financial centre.

The city has also become a magnet for the poor, who wish to be a part of the newly booming India, but most arrive to find the streets are paved with beggars and not the gold they had been led to believe. Most find themselves joining the 7 million people that make up the slum dwellers of Mumbai. They have no legal rights to housing, and any dwelling erected that extends a slum without permission means they are at risk from the authorities bulldozers with little warning.

The intensity of this contrast between rich and poor may be summed up by a new high rise apartment block that has been built as a home for one family, and is believed to have cost $2billion. Mukesh Ambani – Chairman of Reliance and India's Richest Resident – has built himself the world's most expensive home. Amongst its many luxuries, it has six floors for parking up to 168 imported, luxury cars. From the upper floors it looks down on the millions of poor that make up Mumbai's slum community.

The largest of these slums is Dharavi, which is home to 1 million people living within one square mile, and one of the most densely populated places on the planet. It is Asia's largest slum and sits upon some very valuable real estate indeed.

Plans to redevelop Dharavi are in the advanced stages and could turn a $5 billion profit to the developers. It will also be the largest displacement of people in Mumbai's history. Only those who can prove they have lived there for over 10 years will receive compensation of around $5000, and as many as 500,000 will be displaced and receive no compensation at all.

The area of present-day Dharavi was predominantly mangrove swamp until the late 19th century, inhabited by Koli people, who were mainly farmers and fishermen. However, the fishing industry disappeared when the swamp areas were filled in, but the newly drained marshes provided space for new communities to move into.

Migrants from Gujarat established a potter's colony, and Maharashtrian tanners migrated to Dharavi and set up the leather tanning industry. Other artisans, like the embroidery workers from Uttar Pradesh, started the ready-made garments trade adjacent to Dharavi, and hastened the process of joining separate islands into one long, tapered mass. Dharavi's first school was constructed in 1924; it remained the only school of Dharavi, for the next four decades.

The majority of the residents of Dharavi are Dalits but various other castes and tribes are also present including a small number of Christians, Muslims and Buddhists.

In addition to the traditional pottery and textile industries in Dharavi, there is an increasingly large recycling industry, processing recyclable waste from other parts of Mumbai. In fact Dharavi is responsible for recycling 80% of Mumbai's plastic. The district has an estimated 5000 businesses and 15,000 single-room factories, though few if any are registered with the Government and therefore technically trade illegally.

Wages in Dharavi are above the national average and though

many will struggle to earn more than a few pounds a day, it also boasts a few millionaires who have taken advantage of this tax free ghetto.

There have been many plans since 1997 to redevelop Dharavi. The latest urban redevelopment plan proposed for the Dharavi area would be managed by American-trained architect, Mukesh Mehta. The plan involves the construction of 30,000,000 square feet (2,800,000 m²) of housing, schools, parks and roads to serve the existing families residing in the surrounding area, along with 40,000,000 square feet (3,700,000 m²) of residential and commercial space for sale. There has been significant local opposition to the plans, largely because existing residents are due to receive only 225 square feet (20.9 m²) of land each. Furthermore, only those families who lived in the area before the year 2000 are heading for resettlement. It is believed that as many as 500,000 people will not qualify leading to the largest displacement of people in Mumbai's history. Concerns have also been raised by residents who fear that some of their small businesses in the 'informal' sector may not be relocated under the redevelopment plan. The government has said that it will only legalise and relocate industries that are not 'polluting.' This is a worrying time for the potters we work with.

It has been estimated that 5 million people in Mumbai still have no access to a toilet and instead make use of open sewers and in the case of Dharavi, make use of Mahim Creek, a local river, which is widely used by local residents for urination and defecation, leading to the spread of contagious disease. This scarcity of toilet facilities leads to severe problems with public health, due in turn to the fact that most housing and 90% of the commercial units in Dharavi are illegal. As of November 2006 there was only one toilet per 1,440 residents in Dharavi. The area also suffers from problems with inadequate drinking water supply as most water and indeed electricity is illegally connected.

The Dharavi slum was made famous by Danny Boyle's film, Slum Dog Millionaire and was the subject of a recent Channel 4 documentary, where Kevin Mcloud, of Grand Designs fame, lived for two weeks to experience life there first hand. The documentary recorded that the slum has recently gained interest from town planners and architects due to its low crime rate, high employment and sense of community.

Prince Charles visited the slum in 2003 and has been a keen advocate for their sense of enterprise and community ever since, referring to it at a number of functions for leading architects. Quite what he would say if the "monstrous carbuncle" was on his door step I am unsure.

In my opinion, the plans to redevelop Dharavi would be a disaster for its residents and re-housing them in high rise flats will destroy the amazing sense of community that they currently possess. We have a precedent in this country, since the 1950's, of creating our own ghettos by providing similar vertical occupancies in place of terraced houses and the subsequent death of communities. I am no architect or town planner but I know how cheaply the present accommodation could be improved by providing three story houses from locally sourced bricks costing a few pence each and still creating land space for new developments. At the same time, the businesses could be legitimised which would then incur tax liability, and bring revenue into the local government.

Under David Cameron, the current British Prime Minister's ideas for 'Big Society,' we are being encouraged to look at a greater community spirit that requires less government involvement or support, creates enterprise and reduces crime, and provides a safe and sustainable society. Dharavi is all of this and more and yet within a year it may cease to exist. The land, in the greedy eyes of the developers, is simply too valuable to consider things as unprofitable as community.

A potter's house in the Dharavi slum.

I have now visited Dharavi many times and been amazed at the children who emerge from their shacks wearing gleaming school uniforms and speak near perfect English, and aspire to achieve great things for themselves and their families.

I was chatting with one of the potters' daughters recently and asked what she would like to do when she finished her studies. 'I would like to be an air hostess,' she replied. It occurred to me later that she would be the first person in their family, for at least the last three generations that did not go on to work in the family business. It would also mean that she would be away from home, breaking the family unit, and joining an industry that adds to the world's air pollution and global warming. In fact she is chasing the Western dream that is moving increasingly quickly to the East. And who can blame her? But I wonder if her family will witness, as we did in the UK, the decline of a community in exchange for materialism. I am unsure if Air India or Jet Airways are yet employing Dalits, but I hope her qualifications will open the doors that she wants them to. And she is lucky. Her parents can afford the expensive fees of a decent school. Many other children over many years have grown up in Mumbai to find the access to an education impossible.

One young man seeking his future in Mumbai was Solomon Missal, a Christian from Orissa who had applied for a job as a clerk and had gained an interview for the post. He travelled by train to Mumbai with high hopes, but soon discovered that the City has highly skilled thieves included in its burgeoning work force. His bag was stolen, along with the address of the potential employer, and he had simply no way of redeeming it. As he sat forlornly at the side of the road, a young man asked him if he needed assistance. Solomon explained his circumstances and in return was offered a room for the night whilst he considered his options. The young man worked for World Vision, an International charity who, amongst other things cared for homeless children rescued from some of the 250,000 children living on Mumbai's streets. With limited options, Solomon offered to work with the young man for his board and lodgings, which was accepted, and he soon began to fall in love with his work and with the street children of Mumbai. His day was mainly centered on the City's many train stations, where the children would eke out a living by begging or scavenging. But it is a dangerous existence, being easy prey to the beggar kings who notoriously will maim or blind children to make them more successful in their trade. But the trains themselves are killers, taking around 4000 lives a year, as people avoid the bridges in an attempt to save time. Many children who make the railway station their homes are killed on the lines as well, as they scavenge scraps that may provide a meager meal or have potential for recycling.

When World Vision eventually cut the budget and Solomon was made redundant, he decided to go on his own. The children were still there and he felt he couldn't leave them, and so began to seek supporters who shared a heart for his work.

Solomon and Sunita Missal and below just a few of the many children that they have rescued from a life on the streets.

I heard about Solomon through a friend and in 2000 arranged to meet him. He is a small man with a big heart and, as by coincidence had recently lost his sole benefactor, I decided immediately that this was someone I wanted to support. He had previously been able to raise money for a boy's home and we both felt a strong sense of God's agenda in bringing us together to develop the work. Over the last 10 years I have seen the children that Solomon and his wife Sunita have adopted grow up and some are now married with jobs. They have a strong Christian faith and have every opportunity available to them in the new booming India. They are incredibly fortunate to have been saved from the potential abuse that so many children fall prey to on the streets of this vast city. It is a model that I endorse and am so keen to expand. This is not a foster home but a family home. The children are adopted for life and for just £200 a month, all the overheads and needs are met for the children and their parents. There are also plenty of trustworthy people who are willing to manage such a home and so I am keen to work with anyone who may consider sponsoring such a worthy cause.

But in 2006, when I first talked to Solomon about the ideas of expanding this work, I had no idea that my own situation at home was about to take a major turn for the worse.

CHAPTER 14

GOING BUST

In 2006, the U.K. was a great place to borrow money. House prices had soared over the previous 10 years and anyone with a bit of equity behind them and a good idea could raise pretty much what they wanted. Being short of ideas has never really been a problem for me, although it has created a few when I have failed to discern how many I could cope with.

Our wholesale business continued to grow successfully, supplying a growing number of brands, including Ted Baker, Fred Perry, Fat Face, Titleist, and many more who we designed, sourced and imported product for. In addition we had secured licenses with Umbro, Ben Sherman, Lonsdale and The Football Association to supply licensed product into retailers throughout the U.K. and Ireland. We were also trying to launch Tough Jeans in the UK, which was an amazing and trendy Hong Kong based brand we had picked up through our office based over there.

To enable us to continue the expansion we had recruited some senior management whose salaries reflected their c.v and our ability to borrow money successfully was becoming a necessity.

Having served our apprenticeship with many 'blue chip' brands over the years I felt we had the team, and the experience to manage our own brand, but knew that launching one from scratch would be an uphill struggle.

One of our brand customers, Kangaroo Poo, had been established by two brothers, then in their 50's, who had taken the business about as far as they felt they could, and an offer of several million pounds to buy the company was on the table from us. The brothers were keen surfers and set up the brand, initially to support their hobby, but had successfully turned it into a very profitable brand trading out of Ilfracombe. During negotiations, we discovered they were Christians and possibly for this reason had failed to negotiate an exclusivity clause whilst we carried out due diligence on the business. It is often the case that acquisitions are poorly kept secrets and when it was revealed that a bid was on the table, another offer for an extra £900,000 emerged, and was understandably accepted. We were not prepared or able to match it and withdrew our offer.

At the same time we were manufacturing for another brand, Weird Fish, who with no natural successor and no management structure, was being run remarkably profitably by a stalwart gentleman of 65 years of age, though he looked and behaved much younger. He agreed to sell us the business for a negotiated sum of £2.3 million, and without wanting to make the same mistake twice, entered into an exclusivity agreement for a period of 12 months whilst we evaluated the business and again, carried out due diligence.

Six months into negotiations and whilst on holiday on the isle of Islay, I received a phone call from the owners accountant saying that the deal was off. Apparently the proprietor had been playing golf whilst staying at his Spanish villa and had decided that he would be 'bored out of his head' without his business, and had decided to carry on. In fairness to him, he then re-launched himself into the business with vigour, opened an online store, and has grown the business at a remarkable rate, and reportedly sold it recently for £15 million. In all honesty I doubt I could have done better, but regretted not having had the opportunity to try.

The costs of acquisitions are considerable and we had spent around £150,000 on legal and accountancy fees in the process.

In 2007 the Fairtrade Foundation launched Fairtrade cotton, and having spent my life in the fashion industry and being a great believer in the Fairtrade foundations ethos I was keen to exploit what I saw, as a real opportunity. I believed that the USP's (unique selling points) of having both Fairtrade and organic cotton, to an increasingly environmentally aware consumer, created an opportunity that was compelling.

We researched the market thoroughly and discovered that 90% of consumers would prefer a product if it were Fairtrade and organic, compared to exactly the same 'conventional' product, but only 10% were prepared to pay more for it. This new breed of 'ethical consumers' were spending a staggering 24.7 billion a year, with Fairtrade sales growing at an impressive 50% year on year. It was clear to us therefore, that the product would need to be price sensitive to be successful, but believed this could be achieved by direct sourcing in India, despite the premium that Fairtrade and organic products carry. In addition it combined our charitable aspirations with our commercial goals and so in 2007 we launched Ascension Clothing, a 'street' fashion range of denims, printed t-shirts, sweats and accessories.

The name and trade mark – Ascension, had come to us via a failed night club launched by my friend Cameron Dante, who had been front man with The World Wide Message Tribe for 8 years. We had invested £27,000 into merchandising product and a further £10,000 in guarantees for the nightclub, which was another hit to the bottom line when the nightclub went bust.

As a Christian, I believe that we are to aim to be good stewards of our own resources, but also that God commissioned us to look after this planet that we have the privilege of sharing with the rest of nature. But rather than share it, we appear to plunder it as if we had a Universe full of spare parts and refills, easily to hand. As India, China, Brazil and Russia all compete to be the super powers of the future, it is clear that we will be unable to encourage them to be less greedy than the West has been and it would smack of hypocrisy to them if we do so. How can you argue that 40 million people in India, and thousands of schools, who do not currently have electricity should stay that way? How can you argue that the vast amount of coal reserves that India and China have should not be converted to cheap energy to provide this most basic of commodities, electricity, essential to the rest of us for our welfare and prosperity. Yet the consequence is increased pollution on an unprecedented scale – surely a classic 'Catch 22' situation.

Our burgeoning population is, and has always been totally dependent on our ability to grow or produce enough food to feed ourselves. It has been said that, with the discovery of fossil fuels as a source of energy, we tapped into the work of the sun stored up millions of years ago and this 'two sun' effect has allowed us to multiply at an unprecedented rate, as fossil fuel-driven machinery, and manufactured fertilizers and pesticides force the earth to yield more and more food per acre.

My research into the ethos of the Fairtrade Foundation and the merits of organic production, prior to the launch of Ascension clothing, encouraged me that the brand did indeed have a moral and ethical message behind it. I was pleased because this was something I had hoped to develop to a greater extent in my business life for some time.

Around 20,000 farmers a year using back-pack sprays in developing countries die from the inhalation of pesticides, and a further one million are hospitalized and 3 million suffer bronchial problems. In America millions of birds die from crop spraying from the air each year. In India, where the spraying of pesticides is by back pack, it is common place to see farmers spraying in the field, sometimes where children play, and whether through poverty or ignorance, face masks are rarely used. In both cases however, further damage is caused to the environment as rain water washes the chemicals into streams and rivers, killing fish, insects, birds and plant life. In addition fertilizers force the ground to produce more growth but put nothing back into the soil requiring more fertilizer in the following season to get the same yield. This leads to a trap for the farmers who are in effect bound to the fertilizer corporations, which leads to spiraling debt and in many cases suicide.

A rural farmer returns after a days work with feed for his buffalo. A day's labour will return him less than .75pence per day.

The number of farmers who have committed suicide in India between 1997 and 2007 now stands at a staggering 182,936. Close to two-thirds of these suicides have occurred in five states (India has 28 states and seven union territories). The Big 5 – Maharashtra, Karnataka, Andhra Pradesh, Madhya Pradesh and Chattisgarh – account for just about a third of the country's population but two-thirds of farmers' suicides. The rate at which farmers are killing themselves in these states is far higher than suicide rates among non-farmers. Farm suicides have also been rising in some other states of the country. What do the farm suicides have in common? Those who have taken their lives were deep in debt, in fact, 82 per cent of all farm households in Andhra Pradesh were in debt by 2001-02.

Spurred on by a desire to combine our commercial aims with our ethical aspirations, we invested around £150,000 into design and product development of Ascension clothing and also the initial stock levels, and a further amount was set aside to market the brand. We felt we were on track with our plans to launch the brand and that all this additional investment could be justified through our existing licensing and wholesale business, Hothouse, where relationships with the major brands seemed strong.

2006 was also the year that a Christian friend of mine, with a marketing background felt that we should explore a merger. We both felt that our combined resources seemed mutually beneficial to each others businesses and began to find ways to develop this. As an indication of his commitment I was given a 25% stake in a business that was about to be floated on the AIM stock market. On the launch date, and having raised £7 million to develop the business, my shares alone were valued at over £2 million but were locked into the business for a further 2 years. To an entrepreneur, this sort of thing can be an adrenalin shot in the arm, and we believed that, whatever we tackled, we would now find the cash to make it work.

Our Creative Director in Hothouse was passionate about trend information and went to great lengths to share his knowledge and research with our brand clients. This was generally well received and after a meeting at Nike European head office, where we successfully presented our trend report with their entire apparel team, I believed we had a commercial product that we could develop. This was confirmed by a subsequent, positive meeting with Puma who confirmed they would make use of our product and we began to work with Manchester University to develop our ideas. The new business was branded Preview Trend and was to be a web-based trend service. We acquired a partnership with the commercial arm of Central St. Martins University in Holborn, one of Europe's leading design Universities, to develop our ideas. 50% of St. Martins' students are from oversees and so our content was to be fed by their alumni, following 3 years of 'real world' experience in industry.

We managed to raise £125,000 of external investment and, being convinced that this was to be 'the big one,' injected a further £350,000 of our own money. We recruited some very talented people to work on the project, but after 18 months of development were aware it needed a further £500,000 to make it fly. There wasn't a single voice of doubt from my advisors, including accountants Baker Tilly and legal firm Halliwells, who all saw great potential in our product. We also recruited an investment company in Mayfair, London, to raise the further £500,000 required via a Private Placement Memorandum, with a view to floating the company on the stock market. It was valued at £2.5 million before it had even traded.

The offer letters were out with the investors in August 2007 and we excitedly anticipated the money coming in, buoyed by the knowledge that the only similar trend service had sold earlier that year for £140 million. But much of business is about luck with timing and our timing was out. During the middle of September, The Northern Rock sought assistance from the bank of England and our fortunes were likewise, about to turn sour. As story after story broke of a crisis in the banking sector, it became impossible for us to raise the money we needed, and worse still, our existing bankers looked to reduce their current exposure. We kept the business going by Julia and I putting even more of our personal money in, but by December 2007 we knew that the situation was beyond our ability to resource, and with the HSBC being bankers to all our business interests and with no further ability to service their loans, we closed the doors on 30 years of business and made our staff redundant.

I remember walking around our offices and looking at the empty desks. Each member of staff had been interviewed and recruited by myself and Julia. Many had been real friends, in and out of the work place. The sense of waste and loss was extremely painful and the associated grief and uncertainty difficult to bear. To lose a job is hard but to involuntarily draw a close on a lifetimes work is harder. Few people would choose to be out of work or out of business and it often leaves a whole in our lives that is difficult to fill. So much of our identity is caught up in what we do. Titles like Managing Director have associated Kudos. The cars we drive and the houses we live in all make up a picture of who we feel we are. But that is so desperately shallow and untrue.

Ironically, it was the Northern Rock that had leant Julia and I £350,000 against our home during this period, on a self assessment basis. It was this kind of reckless lending by the banks and irresponsible borrowing on our part, that was reflected in so very many sectors of business and society that caused us, and many others to fail. If you are wondering what happened to the listed company, by the time I could sell the shares they were valued at £16,000.

Hindsight is a wonderful thing and it is always hard not to feel self recrimination and a desire to 'put the clocks back.' But that is like a gambler saying, 'if only I had backed the other horse,' and as meaningless as the car crash victim saying, 'if only I hadn't driven to work that day.' For all, like us, who have gone bust during this period, take some comfort from the vast organisations that have done likewise. Even Halliwells, the vast firm of solicitors who advised us, currently owe creditors £190 million and are in administration.

Christmas 2007 was enjoyed with a brave face and through gritted teeth. We had, as usual, shared it with all our extended family and over the years our farm has been a very special place for everyone to gather, at that time of year. As Julia packed away the Christmas decorations, we knew it was likely to be for the last time at our lovely farm.

Whilst staying with us that Christmas, Julia's dad, Harry, had mentioned numbness in his arm, though we dismissed it at the time. At 75, he was still fighting fit and regularly cycled 18 miles, or walked up to 20 miles in a day. He was one of life's great characters and much loved by his friends and family for the tales he would tell, both real and embellished and usually with a pint in his hand. Like my own father, he had been a journalist all his working life and had retired to Leek in Staffordshire, so that his wife Barbara and he could be nearer the family.

It was March before he was diagnosed with an aggressive form of brain cancer and for the following 6 months we watch our beloved Harry slowly drift away.

Julia's mother, Barbara had shown an astonishing level of care for her husband and, preferring for Harry to stay at home, Julia and her brother Mark had supported Barbara well and been drawn much closer to each other through this experience. This was some compensation at a devastating time, but it was another bitter blow.

I am not sure if I ever seriously contemplated suicide at this time, but the depth of sadness and loss I felt had caused me to desire life no longer on a number of occasions. Perhaps that is the same thing. It wouldn't have taken much more to tip me over the edge. To be honest I felt betrayed. Every one of our staff got other jobs almost immediately and in some cases we helped to negotiate much better salaries. Members of our management team had set up in competition to us within two days of being made redundant, and even Christian colleagues took advantage of our situation. I also felt betrayed by God. There were just too many 'whys?' I have thought long and hard to see if there were dissenting voices that warned of imminent failure but there were none – none that I could hear anyway. All my advisors from my accountant and solicitor to my management team were all indicating their support.

Is God really unable then to override that? Is he helpless to watch as the train of destruction heads our way? I felt betrayed that he had led me down the garden path. I felt my omnipotent God had become impotent – unable to assist in my moment of greatest need and pain. I am fully aware that you, reading this, may have suffered a greater tragedy than mine – which was primarily a financial one, and if so I hope I could share and understand your grief and that of thousands of others like you.

I also remember feeling broken hearted but at that time only broken in my sense of loss. I have since come to see that differently: For a surgeon to operate on a broken heart will involve risk, danger to the patient and pain in the recovery. This analogy in surgery, being metaphorically and practically clinical, may indicate the spiritual surgery that was necessary on me. If I loved money then I now love money less and if I felt a freedom in my ability to acquire things I have come to adjust to my current inability. But that healing process, if that was what it was, came with the associated pain and a resulting heart that I believe is now more sensitive – perhaps more exposed.

The term 'hit rock bottom' is often used to summarise the lowest point one can reach. But it is the going down, the uncertainty of where the bottom may be and how far you will fall that is so gut-wrenchingly terrifying. If you know in advance how much you will have or where you will be at the end of a process, then you can begin to plan and mentally and practically adjust. When matters are taken out of your hands and the outcome is impossible to predict, then fear is a certain consequence.

One of the most difficult parts of our experience was that God seemed silent throughout. I believe that Julia and I have a strong faith and though it has been tested over the 30 years that we have been Christians and married together – that faith has remained intact. We are not of the persuasion that God speaks audibly in every circumstance or gives foolproof guidance in all situations. In fact I am convinced He does not, in order to allow us to grow and mature and I also believe that risk taking is a part of life and faith and the outcomes are not always determined by us or by God, though He is aware of them at all times.

This silence in adversity is a common theme for believers and has led me to wonder again at the words of Jesus on the cross when he cried 'My God, My God, why have you forsaken me.' Even the son of God cried, 'why?' There are a number of explanations offered but I wonder if for God himself, through His son Jesus, to be able to truly understand our sufferings then he also had to endure them. If, because God is omnipotent, one would argue that he must already know what suffering would be like – perhaps one would also accept that we are not omnipotent, and it is therefore for our sake that He suffered, and so that we cannot say, 'you do not understand what my suffering is like.'

I know that suggests God is far more personal than many people can accept but that *is* the Gospel message, and is there any purpose in believing in a God who is only interested in when things go well for us and 'legs it' at the first sign of trouble? I think not, but it remains true that silence from God is often the enduring and inescapable partner of grief.

C.S. Lewis records that, at the death of his wife through cancer, 'it was as if God had locked and double bolted the doors, and he was on the other side.' But this is not in the nature of God who is the ultimate recycler and promises, in Romans 8 verse 28, to make good of all things for those that love him. I am convinced that God's absence in suffering is only a feeling, however powerful and painful that feeling is, and an inability on our part to see beyond the all encompassing grief. God is not unaware or uncaring, and in time we will see that the great recycler will let nothing go to waste.

I read a lot of Christian books on the subject of loss and grief whilst trying to find some common themes that I could cling onto. Perhaps the most helpful to me and suitably titled was – 'When heaven is silent,' by Ron Dunne. I had heard him speak at the Keswick Convention many years earlier but was unaware that he had suffered huge personal loss.

Ron was an internationally well respected American speaker but in 1975 his son committed suicide. Ron fell into a prolonged period of depression and his book records how he battled with self recrimination and the stigma of being a Pastor, yet had been unable to help his closest family, and inevitably and repeatedly asked the question, 'why?' It was many years later that he was able to write his story but recalls that, after 10 years, when his depression eventually lifted; he realised that he had been asking the wrong question. There may never be an answer to the question 'why,' not on this side of heaven anyway. Instead the question we should ask, he suggests, is 'what's next?'

CHAPTER 15

WHAT I LEARNED WHEN GOD IS SILENT

I mentioned in an earlier chapter that the Message event in 1988 had been redeemed by an old lady who had been refunded £5,000, which she had lost in the Barlow Clowes affair. I omitted to mention that prior to this, and before we were married, Julia had worked and been involved with the sale of a Barlow Clowes product named Portfolio 30. I am not suggesting for a moment that she was responsible for the downfall of the company but the story is worth recording. Julia's employers at the time were D.C Wilson and Co, headed by a very good friend of mine Denis Wilson. Denis was a well known and respected Christian and many of his clients had trusted him with their personal investments and, with Barlow Clowes offering exceptional returns, Denis had likewise entrusted much of his client's savings into the Barlow Clowes fund. The collapse of the company was a devastating time for Denis and his family and the inevitable recrimination and finger pointing was hard to bear. He is one of the few people I know personally that has suffered similar levels of loss as ourselves, and experienced the combined angst of seeking spiritual explanations and practical solutions to the problems that ensue.

I met Denis for dinner recently. He is now in his 80's but maintains great wit and character and provides excellent company combined with a penchant for very strong Manhattan's. Several years ago his beloved wife Irene died after a prolonged period of illness, so it was encouraging to see someone with faith and hope intact, despite the trials that life has thrown at him. In particular Denis states that the loss of his business was the best thing that could have happened to him. He believes that the lessons he learned and the value systems he developed were aided by the collapse of his business and – through that most testing time.

I am not sure that I can say that yet. In all honesty I would have preferred to have sold my business or the shares when they had a value and would now be working on the charity with my house and financial resources intact. But that is to exclude what I truly believe, and that is that God is interested in your heart with one overriding desire for us, that we 'be conformed to the image of His son,' as recorded in Romans 8 v 29. It is for others to say whether that has happened to me through my circumstances but I know it is his will that it should, and I also know that my passion for the poor, the projects I am involved in and the audience I now engage with, are all greater because of those difficult circumstances. I am not sure that I have the courage to vote for the path that God has for us but I am not alone. Jesus prayed fervently that he may avoid the cup of suffering that awaited him. But it was for a greater good that he suffered and surrendered to God's will, with the words; 'Yet not my will but yours be done.'

Why should *we* assume that following Christ should be pain free when the Bible often indicates otherwise? Yet our society's safety nets, our ranking amongst the world's wealthiest nations and our opportunities all influence us to think that our provisions are a right and not a privilege, all of which are not available to the vast majority of the world's population.

Many of us live a form of Western Christianity rather than a biblical one. By that I mean that we are absorbed into the world's systems of buying and selling and getting and keeping, which often conflict with God's Kingdom system of sewing and reaping and giving and receiving. With such emphasis in society today on materialism and the supposed happiness and security that can offer, it is not surprising that few of us would choose to have less materially – to achieve more spiritually, and most of us would ignore the teaching that we are to seek first *His* kingdom *and* all these things will be added unto us, and the clear command of – 'do not store up for yourselves treasures on earth.' Those parts of me that wish to put the clock back and do it differently so that we didn't suffer the losses, may well be working against the will of God. I am not suggesting that God caused the losses but that he allowed them for a greater good, and I do believe there is a difference. If we measure blessings by merely material things then we shun those things which God sees as having a greater value. Should we too not value integrity, honesty, compassion, bravery, generosity and love higher than money? But many of us, under pressure and if we are honest, would rather take the cash.

Our Westernised Christianity also leads us to see trials and difficulties in an unbiblical way. Jesus states; 'In this world you will have trouble.' Too right! The book of Revelation 21 verse 4 predicts a time when men will share the dwelling place of God and at such time 'there will be no more death or mourning or crying or pain.' – Until that time folks bad things happens. The bible records in Rom 8 v 20-21 – 'For the creation was subjected to frustration' – and has not yet been fully liberated 'from its bondage to decay.' Until that time we are living as if in the gap and so we get sick, businesses fail, tsunamis happen, crime, and that old fashioned word sin is a constant. Perhaps the answer is to enjoy the moment as much as possible knowing that perfection is not ours at this time and find joy in small things and in the God who made them. I have found comfort in a God who is wonderfully able to meet me in small, intimate and almost insignificant answers whilst the big ones remain unanswered. Meditation is a central theme of all religions and the quieting of the mind will give space to solving minor mysteries as in 'where have I left my keys?' as much as in major solutions. But it is also the emptying of the mind that gives God space to enter your thoughts.

When James says, in James 1 v 2; 'consider it pure joy when you face various trials,' we need to remember that he is not saying that the trials are to be encouraged but that we should expect a positive outcome – that outcome brings greater perseverance, maturity and completeness. But he is saying *when*, and not *if* trials happen.

At the time of the Boxing Day Tsunami in 2004, I recall the Arch Bishop of Canterbury saying that he had no answers – at least of a spiritual nature, to explain the devastation or death that had been inflicted upon 500,000 people. If one of the great academics of the Anglican Church struggled then, what hope for the rest of us?

As a direct result of the tsunami I became involved with a small slum community and in a very short while their children will receive an education where before there was none. This is a miniscule example of God making good from bad but will combine with a multitude of similar acts that came in response to the disaster. Is that all we can say then, that as I stated before, 'that God is the ultimate recycler of bad things into good?'

The earthquake in Japan struck recently with the loss of many lives and similar devastation, as in the 2004 tsunami in Indonesia. Again the world asks 'why?' We are astonished by the magnitude of the disaster but I have to believe that God cares as much if it were one life lost as 1 million lives affected. Jesus wept at the death of his friend Lazarus and also over the whole city of Jerusalem. Death is a consequence of life, and a family drawn closer together through the death of a loved one is as valuable to an infinite God as a nation drawn closer to another through a tsunami disaster. We cannot judge God by the scale of the disaster. Our fate in death, whether life is long or short for us remains the same. In the scale of eternity, perhaps then, that will make sense, but in a broken world waiting to be redeemed disaster remains our prickly bed fellow.

I think I have learnt something about prayer as well. A wonderful verse in Revelation 8 v 4 records there was silence in heaven, then; 'The smoke of the incense, together with the prayers of the saints, went up before God from the angel's hand.' The silence that often accompanies prayer is not an act of apathy or indifference on God's part but one that requires submission to His timing and awareness that a process of change that accompanies an answer will not be rushed. Perhaps one of the greatest tests and confirmations of our faith is to be able to accept the answer 'no' to our prayers or to suffer prolonged silence and still continue to believe.

When Shadrach, Meshach and Abednego were faced with worshiping an idol or death in a fiery furnace they respond with remarkable courage and conviction;

Dan 3:17-18 'If we are thrown into the blazing furnace, the God we serve is able to save us from it, and he will rescue us from your hand, O king. But even if he does not, we want you to know, O king, that we will not serve your gods or worship the image of gold you have set up.'

They state that they believe that God is able and willing to miraculously save them but show a deeper faith in that 'even if He does not – we will not serve your God's.' – Even if things do not turn out the way I want I will maintain my faith. That is not a blind faith in that they have given up their sanity but a faith in an unseen outcome, the owner of which they will continue to trust.

The biblical example of Joseph records that he suffered betrayal by his brothers, and experienced the pit and the prison before he could rule in the palace. This and many stories like it do not randomly appear in the Bible for no reason, but outline the truth and reality of life, whilst detailing God's nature and outcomes through trials. It was the period of removal from his job as humble shepherd and the place of favoritism from his father, to one of rejection by his brothers – and imprisonment twice – and both times innocently, that makes this story important. He resisted sexual temptation from his master's wife and eventually went on to govern Egypt in a time of great famine. Character building and testing periods of our lives define who we really are, and if our integrity will remain intact. Daniel's integrity was tested as he was thrown into the lion's den, and Meshach, Shadrach and Abednego as they were thrown into the furnace. Jesus likewise was tested as he faced the cross along with a million unnamed and unrecorded Saints who have been likewise tested in differing ways.

Billy Graham, arguably the world's greatest evangelist of the last century was once asked what he thought was the meaning of life. He answered that he believed 'life is a test.' And who am I to disagree?

CHAPTER 16

JULIA'S STORY

I have asked Julia to tell her own story in this next chapter so here it is;

'Simon said he was going to record our story, I said PLEASE tell the whole thing, include the bad stuff, the detail that makes this an honest story, so that when others read it they don't just see an account of us triumphing over hard times, lessons learned and all safe and sound in Gods pen – because forgive me that is how we often portray our lives to each other. It's as if we dare not admit that we have been on the brink of binning our faith, our marriage – perhaps for some, even life itself – it's like we don't believe that God has a strong enough case going to be able to defend himself! Rubbish, its only when we remove the smiley, "I'm Fine" layers, bit by bit – (or maybe God does that?) and we open ourselves up to others, that we begin to deserve the help that we need to get through this particular bit of life. If we never peel back the facade, let the smile slip, how on earth are our friends and those around me going to know I need help? Churches and Christian gatherings are full of smiley happy faces – are they really smiling – inside?

I said to Simon, tell them about me – about us – how we wept with fear and desperation, sometimes waking with terrible night terrors, how I shouted, pleaded, hated , felt betrayed and alone – he said "You tell them."

Where do I start, how far back do I go?

Where did it all begin to go wrong – or did it?

I have a way of thinking that I battle with all of the time – that is that I am being punished for behaving badly, for not getting my Christian behaviour right for being, albeit unknowingly, disobedient. It's not like I killed someone, had an affair or stole something that I can look back to and say that's when it all began. Not at all.

I have to seriously fight to dispel my personal myth that God is cross with me and He is doing this. That is not how my God works. Time after time I am reminded that my God loves me like my Dad loved me – only better. My Dad would have done anything for me to make me happy. I still vividly remember the day when my heart had been broken and I arrived back at my family home, 47 Seal Road, Bramhall, after being looked after and loved by my friends Deb and Ian for a few days. There on the front doorstep – front door open was my Dad. No words, there was nothing to be said, just a massive big, from the bottom of his heart HUG. I wish I could have more of those hugs.

Jeremiah tells us that God says; "He knows the plans He has for us and they are for our good and not for evil, and that He has known me since I was in my mother's womb," so when I wake in the middle of the night with my heart pounding and an indescribable terror, there *is* a purpose and it will be well.

The local Anglican Ministers husband wrote in the church magazine recently; "Did Jesus have to die? Strictly speaking no, because He could have chosen to avoid it, nor did He chose to die, *But* He did chose to put Himself in a place where death was the consequence as that was the only way God could be revealed in His true, self giving nature, and more than that, His actions gave us the perfect example of Christian discipleship."

During the years when the business was doing well, life was comfortable materially. There was lots of exciting travel, really posh fast cars and no sense of having any financial worries. When the business needed more cash for expansion, way before things were getting tough, we put our million pound farm house up as security against the loan that the business needed. I remember 2 things happening;

1. We went to the local solicitor to get the papers witnessed and he had to warn us that by doing this we were in danger of losing the house if it all went wrong ... yeh right THAT was not going to happen
2. It was my birthday, a lovely sunny day and I was sitting outside in the sun with the bank manager! I laughingly said "come to see your house, have you Margaret?" never in a million years did I think that we would lose it to the bank.

We didn't count the possible cost of our actions. We didn't measure the risk, or maybe Simon did, but we still felt it was a risk worth taking. You can't live life without risk, you just can not. You'd go nowhere do nothing and be very boring!

As I said, I don't know when the tide started to turn but we had started to realise that things were fast becoming more than difficult at the start of 2007. I had worked in the business for 20 years, I loved the work and I loved, I mean loved, the people I worked with. We had a very low staff turnover particularly for the trade we were in – the fashion business. I like to believe that people were content. It meant that we all knew each other very well and were close.

When it came to pay day and the business didn't have the funds to meet the salaries, it was not a hard decision to make – we lent the business money to pay salaries. Nor was it a hard decision to make when again the business didn't have the funds to meet the value of a crucial bill, we lent again.

The decision did become harder as the pot got lower as month by month we plundered all that we had, policies, endowments, anything that we could raise money against we did. But there was no apparent alternative; we still believed we were doing the right thing, so the loans continued until there was nothing left. No money, no ideas, no second or third chances, no more plans or clever ways to get us out of this hole. And a hole it was, I began to despair, money is a great divider and it was doing its best to divide! It was succeeding.

It was important, looking back, to recognise that as this point we had run out of the ability to DO anything, we just HAD to rely on God. It wasn't like I was peaceful and just smiling saying; I know my God will get us through, I knew that bad things were happening and did happen to Christians. They do get cancer – go bust – die. So the key isn't whether they happen – it's how we respond when they do, or is it how we respond after they do – who knows? I had a choice, of course I did, hang on to God or turn away. But what was the point in turning away, where would I go, what would I do?

The pain of telling people that it was over, there would be no more paydays, no more jobs – it was OVER was intense and heart breaking . We had been able to give them hope before, now we couldn't. These precious friends, whom we had worked with for so many years, were no longer in paid work.

I felt desolate, hurt and frightened – what next? The things I had held as so dear, friendship, being part of people's lives, being popular, were all jeopardised. I felt alone despised and unpopular. Especially so when we received an anonymous text message from someone who felt so embittered that they had gone out and bought a sim card, just so they could be as horrid as they wanted to without me knowing who they were. It cut me deeply as I did know who it was and he had worked with us for the past 25 years.

The house was on the market, it was Christmas and my dad was standing by the Aga in the kitchen one morning. He mentioned that his arm had felt a bit numb. None of us realised just how ominous that seemingly innocuous symptom was to be. Three months later it was eventually diagnosed as a Grade 4 Glioblastoma Multiforme brain tumour – the most aggressive it could be in the deepest most untreatable part of my Dads brain. Dad died 6 months later.

For so much of this time I hadn't known how to pray any more, there were so many prayers and they seemed unanswered. Sometimes all I could do was to scramble on to God's knee and sit there, with His arms around me. So, my Dad, my house, my money, some friends, my pride – GONE . Why ME God why me? Why only me?

I was on welcome duty at church one Sunday, (I couldn't always face church as I mostly just stood or sat there with tears streaming down my face, and a friend holding my hand) and this lady came in. I hadn't met her before but we soon got talking. We opened up to each other very quickly and within 5 minutes I learned that she and her husband had recently lost their business, their home their cars and had even despaired to the point of suicide. On top of that her dad had died from a brain tumour. I asked, although I pretty well knew the answer, "what type of brain tumour?" It was the exact, identical tumour that had so savagely taken my Dad. I knew then and there that my Heavenly Father had heard my cries, it wasn't JUST me, and I was not alone in this experience.

Human nature, well my human nature anyway – spends far too much time looking at other people and convincing itself that other people don't have the same burdens, the same tough stuff – it's much easier for them! That is a lie.

Today I sit here writing this with no idea where we will live in 6 months, nor how we will afford to rent or buy, but I have to believe that God knows. He hasn't failed to provide for us so far, it's just that He hasn't chosen to provide for us the way we wanted Him to!

If I focus on what I haven't got and what I don't know, I will most surely rob myself of the joy of this day.'
Julia

*Julia and a very excited group of children
on their first ever visit to the seaside.*

CHAPTER 17

GRACE

In January 2008 I found myself on my knees scrubbing the kitchen floor. This is not quite as impressive as it sounds as I have only done it once and probably won't do it again. But it well reflected my circumstances as I saw it, both literally and metaphorically. We had been asked by the HSBC, quite politely, to put the house on the market as our personal guarantees required, and we had no option other than to oblige. There would still be a shortfall owed to the bank, even after our family home was sold, but we understood that the bank accepted that – in their words – 'you can't get blood out of a stone,' and therefore understood that they would have to forgive the balance.

There are always a multitude of people who are worse off than I was that morning. I had my health and my wife had stuck with me through a very difficult time. Our children likewise were fit and well and we had no reason to think they didn't have good futures ahead of them. But sometimes all that is lost in grief and that morning my soul was not brave enough to look up and count my blessings.

The house had initially been on the market for £1.1 million but as the market was deteriorating we dropped it by £100,000. It is a beautiful 16th century farmhouse situated in the Peak District National Park, with 12 acres of land and the best views in Whaley Bridge. It had been our home for 20 years and we had seen our children grow up and of course had many wonderful memories of our time there. The land has seen us indulge our love of animals with Highland Cattle that we have bred, along with chickens and geese and my new enthusiasm for Saddleback pigs and Julia's childhood infatuation with horses which have graced our fields. To lose all of this was difficult to bear.

The Aston Martin and the Lexus had already gone and after a flutter of regret would soon be forgotten, but the home is often where the heart is, whether that is a healthy place for it to be or not – it is still a harder burden to shed.

The phone rang as I was about my menial task of scrubbing and Julia spoke to the Estate Agent who informed her that a couple were visiting the area from London and wanted to view the property at short notice. We had received limited interest in the property recently and our expectations were not high. In addition, it was difficult to be enthusiastic about selling our home with no obvious place to go. Julia showed a couple, who we judged to be in their mid fifties, round the property and I saw them for no more than 30 seconds when they peeped into the kitchen and apologised for coming without proper notice, but expressed how much they liked the house. Our expectations however remained modest.

On the following Monday, they again asked to visit the house and explained that they felt this was where they would like to retire, were willing to pay the asking price but couldn't leave their current work commitments for a further 3 years. To Julia's astonishment they then asked her if we would consider living in the house for a nominal rent until they retired. For reasons that have never been clear to me, she said she didn't think so but assured them that we would discuss it.

I managed to speak to the man before he flew back to London and was particularly curious to know what was meant by 'a nominal rent.' 'I was thinking of something like £500,' he said. I felt encouraged. You can't rent a terraced house in Whaley Bridge for £500 a month.

We agreed to accept the offer, though in my battered mental state I expected it to fall through. It turned out that he was a senior partner in a large legal firm. We also discovered that his wife was an Anglican Curate where he was also a Church Warden.

As discussions developed I began to realise that he was very excited about this arrangement and felt it was as mutually perfect for them as it was for us. I decided that I must be dealing with an angel and considered I would chance my arm. We had already explained our personal circumstances and the issues with the business failure so I called him and suggested that, as it was clear that they weren't proposing this arrangement for the money – and dared to suggest that it looked like they had plenty – would they consider a nominal rent. 'What are you thinking,' he replied, '£50 to £100 a month?' £50 would be great,' I said, then held my breath. He agreed, and we have lived in a £1 million farm house in the country for £12.50 a week for 3 years and then have a further 2 year extension at the same rate. In addition they have become firm friends and the best landlords you could imagine. Every time they visit the area we arrange to go to a local pub and they always insist on paying. They are responsible for maintaining the property and have redecorated the outside of the house and the barns and repaired sections of stone walls which is all a weight off my shoulders. They even invited us to stay at their property in France last summer.

May I ask you to consider something in all seriousness? How many people in a recession have £1 million disposable income and don't want a return on their investment, also knowing that house prices are likely to go down? How many people would trust a tenant that they don't know to maintain their property virtually rent free? Under these circumstances how many people would feel that they too were the beneficiaries of good fortune under the arrangement, as these buyers genuinely did? Can you think of one – honestly? I believe there is only one and God found him. How else can you explain such remarkable good fortune?

We all experience grace on a daily basis. It is the mysterious and old fashioned word that every one of all faiths or none appreciates if they were to see it, and is a corner stone of all things good, but we all, rarely recognise it. For the first time in my life I felt grace deeply. With no resources of my own or ability to manipulate a situation, God stepped in. As Paul the Apostle wrote 2000 years ago, 'His grace is sufficient for me,' and I said Amen.

CHAPTER 18

AN EDUCATION IN EDUCATION

Julia has worked with me, on and off, for all of our married life, apart from a brief spell in the early years and whilst our children were growing up. It is not something that I would recommend if asked, but I think we have been a very good, if on a few occasions, volatile partnership. Spending so much time together can dampen the romantic spark, and it is difficult to partition the working and marital relationship at home. However we have learned to have specific roles that hopefully play to our strengths and Julia remains my most valuable asset, my harshest critic and my best friend.

Our remaining money was running out when Julia managed to get a job as an administrative manager at a marketing company nearby. In the mean time a former buyer in Mike Ashley's Empire, he of Sports Division fame, had contacted me to discuss my ideas on forming an ethical bag business. We had supplied him with 500,000 England hats during the World Cup and knew him to be a likeable but judicious business man. With limited options I decided to give it a go and we had modest success supplying Top Shop, Fat Face and a few other brands with Eco shopping bags.

One small bonus was that we had managed to sell the remains of the Ascension Clothing business to newly floated e-commerce retailer Adili, and with the modest amount from the sale were just managing to keep our heads above water.

As I mentioned earlier, we had adopted the name Ascension following the closure of Cameron Dante's night club of the same name. Cameron and his wife Tori and their delightful daughters, Romani and Teaha, had stayed with us in Whaley Bridge on a number of occasions and I was intrigued to see Cameron emerge from being a night club manager to become a successful salesman. His first job was with Pitney Bose, where he rushed through the ranks to become one of their most successful salesmen, and was then head hunted by the Dutch printing company Oce, who specialise in environmentally friendly printers. Cameron focused on supplying schools, which are a major consumer of printed materials and as such had become a bit of an expert on the Government's sustainable schools policy. He was convinced that there were mutual opportunities for us to work together in the education sector, and I eventually decided that his ideas had some merit and we formed a new company to further develop them.

I was happy to let Cameron develop the business plan and he soon managed to get financial support from a number of investors including B.T, Tesco, Mouchel, the RBS and Microsoft.

Prime Minister Gordon Brown had begun a new initiative called Shine, with the mantra 'every child has a talent,' and which was managed by the Talent and Enterprise Taskforce within the Department for Education. Following a meeting with High Peak M.P. Tom Levitt we soon found ourselves invited to an entrepreneur's garden party at No. 10 to meet the Prime Minister. Never one to miss an opportunity, I took a sample of an 'Eco' cotton shopper that had been designed by a local primary school and, much to the envy of other visitors, whipped it out in time to get a photo of myself and the Prime Minister viewing the bag. In addition we managed to 'collar' Jim Knight, the Minister for schools, who promised a subsequent meeting to discuss our ideas.

Our plan was to have a national competition for young people who would design an Eco shopper as part of the Shine initiative. The winning design would be sold in Tesco. Within the project we structured reasons why the environmental elements of design and sourcing were important and our corporate partners were able to add their 'wise words' and be seen to be part of a project that engaged young people in considering environmental and ethical issues within education. To that end I was happy with the business model but confess to being out of my comfort zone and a long way from my background in fashion wholesaling.

A rather bemused looking Prime Minister viewing the Hawthorne / Dante Eco bag.

The judging panel was selected from senior people within our corporate partners plus designer Cath Kidston. The winning design was chosen along with several runners up and we were successful in having the outcome televised on the BBC's regional and national television, and the winner visiting No. 10 to meet the Prime Minister at a prestigious youth event along with dance band Diversity, and various other celebrities.

We wanted to have a measurable outcome from the year's events and so decided to present our findings at a meeting at the QE2 Conference Centre in Westminster. In November 2008 we secured 500 paying delegates and had no less than three Cabinet Ministers and the Deputy Speaker of the House of Commons as guest contributors. Our audience was made up of a billionaire, education heads, leaders of local authorities, captains of industry and, to make it more interesting, a significant number of young people from deprived areas.

Following the success of the event, we were invited to the Speakers Rooms in the House of Commons with other collaborators on the Shine project, and had reason to think that we had ticked our governmental and corporate partners boxes well enough to justify the champagne we were being offered.

Our income stream was beginning to grow and a modest salary was affordable, and we felt confident in opening smart and modern offices in Cheadle. Cameron had put his previous experience into recruiting and training a sales team and our client and Government relationships continued to grow. But if I have learnt anything in recent years it is that life can be unpredictable. I can think of other, more descriptive and colourful words to describe my recent past but suffice to say our project came to an untimely end when the Government's spending cuts terminated the Shine initiative, to which we had been joined at the hip. We were heavily committed to the following year's project and had already made a significant financial investment so the premature demise of yet another promising business felt like opening an old wound.

I have sometimes wondered if the term entrepreneur really means: – a business man that can't focus – or perhaps worse, one who gets bored easily. Great entrepreneurs like Richard Branson or the various investors on Dragons Den, seem to switch from one totally unrelated opportunity to another and almost always seem to come out on the other side, unscathed, and with a healthy profit. Closer investigation into their auto biographies shows this isn't true. Most entrepreneurs will have a list of failures alongside their successes and need deep pockets to see their success delivered. Indeed, it is said that most American Chief Executives will not be seriously considered for a post unless they have a number of failures behind them and that they have learnt from, and can therefore avoid in any future assignment. The debtor's jail is thankfully, long since a thing of the past and, like our American cousins, the UK is more open to the idea of supporting and understanding failure as part of a process and reducing the associated stigma that in the past has accompanied it.

One in ten new-start businesses fail and a similar number of investors or business angels will experience seeing no return on their money by investing in new-starts or ideas. So perhaps, to make a mistake is forgivable, even acceptable, mistakes and failure are all a part of the learning process, just make sure you don't keep repeating the same ones.

In Philippians Chapter 3 verses13 to14, Paul writes:

'But one thing I do: Forgetting what is behind and straining towards what is ahead, I press on towards the goal to win the prize for which God has called me heavenwards in Christ Jesus.'

Sometimes failures serves the purpose of focusing towards that 'one thing' that Paul talks about and setting aside things of lesser value for those that really count. His own testimony is riddled with trials and difficulties and a fair few failures.

In 2 Corinthians chapter 1 and verses 8 to 10 Paul writes:

'We do not want you to be uninformed, brothers, about the hardships we suffered in the province of Asia. We were under great pressure, far beyond our ability to endure, so that we despaired even of life. Indeed, in our hearts we felt the sentence of death. But this happened that we might not rely on ourselves but on God, who raises the dead. He has delivered us from such a deadly peril, and he will deliver us. On him we have set our hope that he will continue to deliver us.'

His analysis was that there was a purpose in his suffering and that was; that he might learn to trust in God and not rely on his own resources.

Whilst travelling as a prisoner aboard a sailing ship and following a mighty storm that threatened to sink them, Paul writes in Acts 27 verse 20:

'When neither sun nor stars appeared for many days and the storm continued raging, we finally gave up all hope of being saved.'

He records that the situation felt hopeless. Now that's not something that is taught very often from the pulpit. But the Bible is remarkably honest about the difficulties that life will throw at us. Almost every chapter is littered with death, grief, pain and suffering and, like an artists palette, sits necessarily alongside the brighter colours of joy, happiness, contentment and success. Maybe, as I suggested earlier – our problem is that we live a Westernised form of Christianity, and not a biblical one. We are so rooted in the expectation of a pampered and privileged life, and sit so comfortably at the pinnacle of the World's wealth that we can no longer relate to scripture or indeed to the billions of people on the planet for whom life is not so generous.

No one in his right mind is going to seek suffering, but no one who understands scripture should be shocked when our own measure of loss is woven into the tapestry of our lives. God is the ultimate recycler. Nothing goes to waste and all our rubbish, dross and misery will, like compost to a rose, bloom into something brilliant in it's time.

CHAPTER 19

A NEW DIRECTION

Steve Chalke is a Baptist Minister, but perhaps better known for his work with his charity, The Oasis Trust. He holds the Guinness Book of records, twice, for the largest amount of money raised at the London Marathon; he is an author of over 40 books, manages 12 Academies and is an International speaker. He is also the United Nations special advisor on people trafficking.

In 2006 Steve had a day care centre for under privileged children in Mumbai. One day, two children who had attended regularly failed to show up and his team visited their home to enquire after them. They discovered that their father had sold them for $10 each. Steve was so upset by this that he formed the charity, Stop the Traffic. He discovered that, according to the United Nations, there are 27 million people who have been trafficked into modern day slavery.

In 2005 Steve had a day care centre for under-privileged children in Mumbai. One day, two children who had attended regularly failed to show up and his team visited their home to enquire after them. They discovered that their father had sold them for $10 each. Steve was so upset by this that he formed the charity, Stop the Traffik. He discovered that, according to the United Nations, there are 27 million people who have been trafficked into modern day slavery. He announced all this at a Spring Harvest Council of Management meeting in Dec 2005 where Marion White was also present and was deeply stirred. Steve recommended that she should go out to Mumbai to see the problem of human trafficking in the raw. So in October 2006 she and nine other women, some from her family, and friends including Steve's wife and Michele Hawthorne went out there.

In Jan/Feb 2007 Marion White planned to do a small tour around England to highlight the massive evil of human trafficking. Marion's brother, Paul Field, a Christian singer/songwriter was simultaneously writing a musical called Cargo about slavery past and present to coincide with the 200th Anniversary of the end of the Transatlantic Slave Trade so they combined forces and the same women who had travelled to India helped present a multimedia event. A young man, trained as an opera singer and part of the church that Rob and Marion White attended, called Ben Cooley, offered to help stage-manage and from there he had the vision to put on an event to call the church to take a stand. So it was that The Stand was planned and in Nov 2008 five thousand five hundred people attended at the NEC in Birmingham. From the interest and response from that event Rob and Marion White and Ben and Deb Cooley were able to form Hope for Justice, a charity focusing on freeing the victims of people-trafficking in Europe, especially in the UK.

Julia and I joined the many people at The Stand for a day of music, and to hear guest speakers from around the world with a shared focus on people trafficking. One of the guest speakers was Joseph De Sousa, the International Director of Operation Mobilisation India, and of the Dalit Freedom Network, known as the DFN. I hope he will forgive me if I say he was not the most charismatic speaker that day, nor can I recall the content of his speech though I am sure it was excellent, but he held something in his hand that was about to change our lives.

I have recorded this chain of events – from Steve to Marion to Ben – as I believe it outlines one of the very real ways that God works, and illustrates how a positive viral effect can happen that can create a movement. Just such a movement of empowered and motivated people is required to tackle the issue of the Dalits today.

For centuries, the Dalit people have been forced to drink from clay cups so as not to contaminate those of a higher caste. Amazingly this practice is still wide spread across many states in India, though they are often now replaced with disposable plastic cups for the same purpose. It is designed to humiliate and reinforces the caste prejudice which remains a reality throughout the country today.

This symbol of oppression had become a focus for the DFN who have produced many tens of thousands of clay cups that they have sold to raise awareness and funds for their charity. I immediately saw potential in the clay cup and determined to explore the possibility of producing a range of clay cup candle pots that we could sell with our retail experience and design skills, to raise money and awareness for our own charity, Life Association.

I visited Joseph De Sousa at his head office in Hyderabad and to seek his approval of the idea and also of Gary Sloan – O.M.'s U.K. Director – at their head office in the Quinta, near Oswestry. Both were fully behind me and saw no conflict with their own work.

I contacted Solomon, the manager of our children's home in Mumbai and asked him to find out where the clay cups were made and also a suitable candle factory that would produce some samples for us. I then visited Mumbai and was delighted to find that the clay cups were made by some of the 100's of potters who live in the Dharavi slum. For more than three generations these potters, who had originally migrated from the neighboring state of Gujarat have been producing clay pots as well as drinking vessels and incense burners.

Potting is traditionally seen as the work of the low caste or Dalits, due to it being considered dirty work and sourced from the earth. It is hard for a Westerner to understand this concept when it would be considered an aspiration to go to say, Central St. Martins University in London to do a degree in ceramics or pottery. But there are many mysteries and oddities associated with India's caste system and it was my good fortune to find such skilled potters that would help me launch our new brand, Dalit Candles.

A skilled potter at work in Dharavi.

One such student who had studied at St. Martins was Stephen Morris. After a year working with me at Hothouse, as an assistant on our design team, Steve had gained a place at the University to study product design. He had left feeling disillusioned with the merit automatically associated with his degree and his seat of learning, but with a strong desire to use his skills for charitable purposes. When we met and discussed our vision for the brand and the paltry salary we could commit to, I was delighted that he still wanted to join us and shun the pursuit of money in favour of the charity.

But how do you start a business with no money? – and with my credit rating shot to pieces I was going to need substantial support to buy the stock, build the web site and pay the wages until the business came into profit. Would anyone really back someone with my recent track record?

My business had failed for a number of reasons but one of them was timing. If I had launched a year earlier I really believe I would have raised the cash to make it work, but by the time we were ready the financial institutions' appetite for lending had dissipated and it was not to be.

One business man had got his timing just right and in 2008 sold his business for seven times the £1.2 million annual earnings the company was then achieving. By his own admission, if it had of been just a few months later it could have been very difficult to complete the sale due to the crash of the financial markets. I met him and explained my vision for the business and discovered that he and his wife passionately shared my heart for the poor and the following day he phoned me to say that they wished to support the launch of our business. By a remarkable stroke of good fortune his experience was in web build and search engine optimisation. God does indeed work in remarkable ways. Not only would they back us – losers, failures, and whatever other negative label I would choose to attach to myself in my lowest moments – they would continue to back us until the business worked and we also become great friends. This, after all, is the Kingdom of God.

By January 2009 I was happy with our range and Steve had come up with some excellent packaging design that also met our 'eco' criteria. Julia left her job and joined us on sales at the same time, and our first consignment was ready to ship shortly afterwards. That is not to imply that that this was without its difficulties. I have long held a saying that I have often quoted to my staff who, from time to time have suffered from supply chain frustrations. That being: 'If it was easy, everyone would be doing it.' None of our supply chain were used to Western standards of quality control or had exported before. We had deliberately chosen factories that are either owned or employ Dalits, and were aware that we had some work to do before we would be knocking on the doors of the major chain stores. However, they were keen to learn and our teething problems that are inevitable in a new business were kept to a minimum, under the circumstances.

More importantly I believe I got the first glimpse of what God wanted from our charity and indeed our lives. As well as the practical work of building 50 schools and children's homes we were to raise awareness of the plight of the Dalits. If we achieved the former, we would rescue 10,000 children a year from poverty and potential exploitation, but that is nothing when 15 million are currently in bonded labour. What is needed is a mass movement of people who will put pressure of Governments around the world to, in turn, put pressure on the Indian Government to enforce their existing laws and abolish the caste system in all its forms.

CHAPTER 20

THE CASTE SYSTEM

The Christian element within the education in our schools is very important to me. If you are a Christian yourself, you will understand why, but if not I would hate my views to sound like an attack on Hinduism, as I believe absolutely in the freedom of religion. But within Hinduism is perpetuated the belief system that men and women are not made equal and that the caste system determines, by birth, your opportunity and future. That surely is a human rights issue. The caste system, I believe, is the greatest human rights issue in the world today, quite simply because of the vast number of people affected. I repeat that I believe absolutely in freedom of religion, as Jesus did. But I also believe that to be able to make an informed choice, then you will need to be educated to be able to make that choice. Central to Hinduism is the caste system which teaches inequality between castes and leads particularly to the oppression of women. For over 3000 years the caste system has meant that millions of people have suffered discrimination and oppression and it continues today, with thousands of acts of violence, persecution and prejudice on a daily basis.

India is the world's largest democracy and the British introduced both the political and judicial system, but they failed to deal with the caste system, which limits the democratic rights of millions that are often forced to vote in line with the will of their high caste masters.

The oxen are yet to be replaced by the tractor in many rural villages.

To understand how this can apply to a country of 1.1 billion people in the 21st century, we have to go back over 3500 years when India was invaded by the Aryan's, who subdued the native or aboriginal people and introduced Hinduism, central to which is the caste system. In the Vedas, written by Manu, the lawgiver, it decrees that God made man according to a certain caste. At the head of the caste system are the Brahmins or priestly caste. Today they number around 4% of the population but still hold most of the power and fortune of India. Below the Brahmins are the Khastriyas or warrior caste, who were the protectors of the Brahmins. Next in line are the Vaisyas or business caste and who work in various forms of commerce. It is largely from these three groups of people that the high and middle class of India come today. Below these three castes are the Sudras, who are the low caste and number around 250 million people. They are employed to serve the other three castes and according to Hinduism, this is the will of the god Vishnu, and as such they will carry out the most menial and dirtiest of jobs. Below this are the untouchables or as they prefer to be called, Dalits, meaning downtrodden and oppressed. They too number around 250 million. They are still sometimes called untouchables and are often expected to cross the road when high caste people are passing in case they 'contaminate' them, and they will often be violently chastised for any breach of their lowly position.

Hinduism states that the four castes originated from four parts of the body of Brahma. The Brahmin priestly caste proceeded from Brahma's head, the Kshatriyas from his arms, the Vaisyas from his thighs and the Sudras from his feet. Far beneath the Sudras are the 'untouchables' or Dalits who were rejects from the social order altogether, being not made by God. (Mahatma Gandhi preferred to call them *Harijans*, meaning the 'Children of God.')

In chai shops and coffee shops Dalits are expected to drink from separate disposable cups so they cannot pollute the vessel. These are often made from clay and are seen broken by the road side but are increasingly being replaced by plastic.

Manu decreed that the Dalits were not made by God, being literally a mistake that should never have happened, and that within society should be considered lower than animals. The holy writings of Hinduism were traditionally read by the Brahmins and written in Sanskrit, but no access was given to the Dalits and is still often denied, and entry to Hindu temples is still prohibited to the Dalits. Indeed Manu wrote in the Vedas that; if a Dalit were even to hear the Sanskrit being spoken, 'they should have molten lead poured into their ears.'

In the south of India, many Dalit communities number up to 90% Christian. This is an amazing and unrecorded fact and indicates a clear rejection of Hinduism amongst this community. If you are told on the one hand that you are recognized by God and therefore society as being lower than an animal, not part of his body and that your lowly position in life is as punishment for acts in a previous life, then on the other that God loves you enough to die for you as the Christian gospel declares, and that your sins are freely forgiven and in God's eyes you are not only equal amongst all men, but that His spirit dwells within you at conversion, then the choice may indeed seem clear. I say this is an unrecorded fact because the Dalit often receives allocated land to live and their children may receive a free, even if basic, education. To declare yourself a Christian removes you from the category of people with this entitlement – a price the Dalit can ill afford. Whether this is a cynical attempt to lock the Dalit into Hinduism or an anomaly of the system isn't clear, but it remains the case that their conversion to Christianity remains unrecorded for this reason.

To visit the major cities of India today, it is easy to believe that the caste system is a thing of the past. Indeed in booming, modern India it is possible to arrive at an International Airport and travel by limousine to a luxury hotel, and be completely isolated from the poverty that is inflicted on the majority of Indians, who have no access, or hope of acquiring the new wealth of India. The truth is that today 1 in 3 of the world's poor live in India, scratching a living on less that 70 pence a day.

In Mumbai, it is still hard to avoid the poverty that is so endemic, and a glance out of most flights into Chatrapati Shiva Airport will witness the sprawling slum of Dharavi, Asia's largest slum, made famous in the film, Slum Dog Millionaire. It is home to one million people who live within a square mile, yet overlooked by more billionaires than London. Seven million people live in such slums in Mumbai and five million have no toilet and limited access to clean water. Yet today, India has the highest number of millionaires in the world. I believe it is impossible to argue that the caste system is not responsible for such a vast gap between the rich and the poor.

Mumbai's modern skyline hides the fact that seven million people still live in slums.

The number of millionaires in India doubled in 2010 yet today, any day, 5000 children will die of malnutrition. That is 1 in 3 of the children that die around the world through lack of proper food. The UN estimate that 1.7 million children in India will die before the age of one – 2.1 million before the age of five. 25% of children are born underweight and the percentage of underweight children age five is 20 times that of the West. If it can afford a space programme, nuclear weapons and currently enjoys 8% growth in GDP, India can afford to feed its poor. The truth is it chooses not to.

The sprawling slum of Dharavi and home to 1 million people.

For 400 years the children of Israel were slaves to the Israelites until God raised Moses to be a voice of the people and lead them to liberation. 200 years ago, William Wilberforce was the voice that led to the end of slavery in this country. More recently Martin Luther King was the voice of the black American and Nelson Mandela was the voice and symbol of black oppression in South Africa and was used to end apartheid. But the caste system is worse than apartheid if only because of the sheer numbers of people affected. Who will be the voice of the Dalits today, who have been oppressed for over 3000 years?

We live in a global community and what we do affects others around the world. Equally, people in other countries may impact us by their environmental or commercial decisions. We can no longer turn a blind eye on the sufferings of others simply because they are not our immediate neighbour, or part of our ethnic group. The world has shrunk and through social networking, the Internet and e-mail, things that were inconceivable a few short years ago can now happen at remarkable speed. In 2011, events unfolded across the Middle East as ordinary people gathered to challenge tyranny and oppression. From Tunisia to Egypt, Oman, Bahrain, Libya, Jordan and Iran, people voted for freedom with their feet and their voices. So too, India's best kept secret must remain secret no longer. The Dalits have not had a voice due to their financial weakness and lack of access to digital media. But that must surely change and developed nations have a responsibility to assist them in achieving liberation now.

Britain, more than any other nation has a moral responsibility to act. This country had the opportunity to end the caste system once and for all when we had the power to do so, but in 1947 we handed over independence to India with the caste system intact. The British Government acquiesced to the Brahmin leaders and the Hindus who opposed change. Even Gandhi, 'the father of India,' though deeply embarrassed by the sufferings of the poor, and working mightily on their behalf and to liberate them from the British rule, chose not to end the caste system. But one voice spoke out at that time for the Dalits. That was Dr. B.R. Ambedkar who was born in central India in the early 1900's. His caste had led to him being forced to take lessons outside the classroom and being thrown out of hotels because of his low caste status. He is known as the champion of the Dalits and even though he had been born into one of the lowest sectors of the Dalit caste system, he overcame the considerable obstacles that were before him to achieve an M.A. Ph.D, D.Sc. and L.L.D. in law from Columbia University in the U.S.A. After returning to India, this brilliant academic became known as the Father of the Indian Constitution. He worked in Government alongside Prime Minister Nero and Gandhi and was alone in pressing for the end of the caste system. He remains a hero to the Dalit people to this day and many villages carry a statue of Ambedkar instead of the more commonly preferred Gandhi seen elsewhere. He is famously quoted as saying 'I was born a Hindu but I will not die a Hindu.' Indeed he converted to Buddhism and denounced Hinduism for the persecution of its own people. To speak out as Ambekar did is not an attack on Hinduism. It is speaking up for human rights which in the 21st century rise above religion on the world stage.

India has no shortage of laws which it is liberal in passing but notoriously fails to enforce. They readily point to their statutes that should protect the rights of the individual but fail to do so. Acts of caste prejudice were made illegal in India more than 50 years ago, but have continued unabated with impunity. A high caste Hindu can get away with murder as I have found in my own experience, by paying a simple bribe. In many cases the low caste can neither afford a defense nor expect a fair trial when corruption is endemic within the judicial system. This is the same system that the British introduced which, again must put a special responsibilty on this country to give the Dalit people a voice. What is written in the Indian Constitution does not work itself out in practice in the villages and towns where Dalit women suffer abuse, humiliation, rape and are often tortured or paraded naked in public.

A justice system is only of any use if an affordable lawyer is available to put forward a case. In a June 2008 report, the United Nations estimated that four billion people in the world live outside the protection of the law. As the report concluded, 'Most people do not live under the shelter of the law' – instead they live in a world in which perpetrators of violence and abuse are unrestrained by the fear of punishment. In the world of the poor, almost every component part of the public justice system including police, defense lawyers, prosecutors, judges and courts work against, not with the poor in providing protection under the law. In the developing world, the average poor person has probably never met a police officer who is not, at best corrupt, or at worse gratuitously brutal.

When a poor person does come into contact with the public justice system beyond the police, it is frequently because he or she has been charged with the crime. With incomes for the global poor hovering around $1 – $2 a day, the average poor person cannot hope to pay legal fees to defend themselves.

According to IJM, International Justice Mission, a US based charity working around the world on behalf of the poor in cases of people trafficking; the problem is made worse by the scarcity of lawyers in the developing world. The average person in the developing world has never met a lawyer in his or her life. In the United States there is approximately one lawyer for every 265 people and in the UK, one for every 402 people. Compare that to Zambia where by contrast there is one lawyer to every 25,667 people or Cambodia where there is one for every 22,402. In India there are only 11 judges to each 1 million people.

Some experts have estimated that at the current rate, it would take 350 years for the courts in Mumbai to hear all the cases on their books. According to the UN Development Programme there are more than 30 million cases pending in Indian courts, and cases remain unresolved for an average of 15 years. Someone who is detained while awaiting trial in India often serves more than the maximum length of his or her prospective sentence even before the trial date is set. The international Centre for Prison Studies at King's College London found that nearly 70 percent of Indian prisoners have never been convicted of any crime. In India, as in many countries in the developing world, judges and magistrates sometimes solicit bribes in exchange for favorable verdicts or, in other cases, to continue the case indefinitely.

Some courts do not even have access to the applicable legal texts, and judges consequently reach decisions without consulting the relevant legal standards. As a result, the idea of legal enforcement is not one of the social mechanisms that most poor people in the developing world consider useful for negotiating a reasonable outcome from the threats of daily life.

In 2007 the J.F.Kennedy Foundation, in partnership with an Indian charity published a report which was featured in the Times of India. It was the result of three years study in the state of Gujarat and took place in over 1600 villages. It reported that in 99.1% of villages inter-caste marriage was forbidden and often violently opposed. To marry someone from another caste, simply for love, would invariably result in beatings or worse and being thrown out of the community. The same report stated that in most schools that did provide an education to the low or outcast, separate seating areas were reserved for Dalits who were also required to eat and drink from separate vessels, and bring their own food into school where other children were fed in the school canteen. But because this survey took place in Gujarat does not in any way imply that the same abuses are not taking place and often more vigorously in other states across India. The India Government has promised education for all but fails to act to back up the promise.

In 2006, a comprehensive study carried out in 565 villages in 11 states revealed that in 28% of villages Dalits were prevented from entering police stations. How can justice be achieved if these people cannot even report a crime? In the same year, according to police records published by the National Crime Records Bureau, there were 27,070 reported cases of violence against Dalits. If we know so many are prevented from reporting cases then how many more would not even bother trying if they believe that the judicial system itself is not on their side. The fact that only 2.3% of cases that ever get to court end up with a conviction is surely enough to discourage most from even trying to seek justice. The same study discovered that in 38% of schools Dalits had to sit separately while eating, public health workers refused to visit the homes of Dalits in 33% of villages, and the post would not be delivered to 23.5% of homes. Even the most basic human right – that of clean drinking water – was denied in 48.4% of villages where the Dalits were segregated and required to drink from separate wells or water pumps due to their untouchability.

India is the world's largest democracy. Democracy is defined by a countries people electing its government by free and fair elections and where the supreme power is vested in the government by the people. But what is free and fair about a system that denies Dalits access to polling booths in 12% of the villages surveyed.

More recent studies carried out in Tamil Nadu in 2008 discovered that higher caste Hindus were given priority in boarding and seating on buses. The study also found that Dalits were not allowed to own male dogs in case their dogs were to mate with a high caste owner's bitch and thus 'contaminate' it. Even in the matter of food there is discrimination. A study carried out in the same year in 521 villages of the more backward states of Bihar, Uttar Pradesh, Tamil Nadu and Andhra Pradesh found that when buying food Dalits were forced to cup hands to receive food and change to avoid touching the seller and were often forced to pay a higher price than the high caste, a cruel twist for the impoverished Dalit.

In 2010, The BBC Crossing Continents programme reported that millions of pounds of money donated by the United Nations to tackling Manual Scavenging in India had been diverted to meet the spiraling costs of putting on the Common Wealth Games, an event that in any case would only ever be accessible to the wealthy. Manual Scavenging is the practice of collecting human excrement by hand and disposing of it and in 90% of cases is carried out by women. It is a practice confined to the Dalits whose children will be expected to carry on this most disgusting and disease ridden occupation after their parents. The wages are too low to afford gloves, face masks or protective clothing and the excrement is usually carried on the head, as is the custom in India, often in leaking cans or buckets. For a pittance they will have a lifetime of stigma, health risks and stench, in a practice that is internationally condemned. Under international pressure the India Government passed a law in 1993 banning the practice of manual scavenging but it has had little effect in rural communities where most of the population lives, and where it fails to address this foul practice that affects an estimated 1 million people.

A large part of our ministry now is to take any opportunity to raise awareness of the issues that the Dalits face and church services usually provide a sympathetic audience. Julia will often take the opportunity to tell a story that she heard, of a female manual scavenger as she went about her work. Dalits have been subject to the most aggressive and dehumanising abuse for centuries. They are born into a culture that devalues them from birth. But they are human beings and according to the Bible; 'made in the image of God.' In glorious defiance of their oppressors the women emerge from shacks in brilliantly coloured and beautiful saris. What ear rings and necklaces they possess will be displayed around their faces, and their children, even when their clothes are almost threadbare, will have their hair in plaits of bows or decorated with a freshly picked flower. Julia's story tells of one woman who carried an old tin can full of human excrement upon her head. She was in her forties and had been about the business of scraping someone else's shit, (forgive me but does another word portray this image better?) She wore a purple sari but the tin was old enough to leak and the contents dripped down onto her beautiful garment. She is a sister, a mother and also someone's daughter. At this point Julia usually completes the story through tears.

One story which similarly pulls at my heart strings at the moment comes following a recent trip to a brick works in India where I desperately want to start an ethical operation that looks after the interests of the workers and provides education for the workers children. The building industry in India is dominated by the mafia and health and safety standards are as rare as an elephant with two trunks. This particular brick works that I was visiting was well organised and employed about 70 workers who produce around 20,000 bricks per day between the months of November and May when the monsoons approach and it is too hot to survive such physical work.

The clay is dug on site and soaked in water pits where rice husks are added to help bind it. The following day, after the water has evaporated the clay is molded into shape in metals casts and laid out in the sun to dry. They are then carried by women, between the ages of approximately 16 and 30, but sometimes as young as 12, to kilns which total around 100,000 bricks. The kilns are built in a pyramid shape and every three feet or so a layer of charcoal is added along with salt, for reasons I am yet to fully understand.

The women carry the bricks on their heads and work in teams of 5 or six. Most of the girls or women were small, I estimate around 5 feet 4 inches tall on average and weighed around 9 stone or about 55 kilos. They load, without assistance from anyone else, around 18 bricks, 3 bricks wide, on boards on their heads and with only a small coil of cloth to aid balance and give some protection.

The bricks each weigh 2.25 kilos so a total of 40 kilos or equivalent to 70% of their body weight unsupported on their heads. This is a remarkable feat of strength and balance but one that comes with considerable risks. The spinal column is under intense pressure when carrying such a burden leading to damage to the nerves and soft tissue around the spine and also wear to the vertebrae. I have shown video evidence of this practice to a senior chiropractor who has confirmed this to be the case and that, in his opinion the main consequence for young women employed in this practice is that they are invalids by the time they are 30, or in such pain that they are unable to continue. This then leads to greater poverty as well as pain in later life. Only Dalits will be expected to carry out this laborious and strenuous work.

A young woman in a Mumbai brickworks carries 18 bricks on her head weighing a staggering 40 kilos.

The children play in the brickworks as the parents go about their business. None receive an education and will sometimes help with small shoveling jobs. One such child, a young girl of around six years of age, had remarkably wild hair that failed to hide her beautiful, if rather dirty face. We nick named her Stig, from the children's story – Stig Of The Dump. We were allowed to enter Stig's home which was a straw hut of about four square meters with no windows and only one entrance. Her father was asleep on the floor as he had been paid the previous day and – as is the custom of the men – on receipt of wages, had consumed enough alcohol to be rendered unconscious. A small baby was asleep in a hammock and a chicken sat in the corner of the hut guarding its clutch of eggs. I fell in love with Stig. But that isn't unusual. If I'd of had my way I would have adopted several thousand of the Dalit children I have met over the years and brought them home to England but in Stig's case at least I would have been wrong to try. Her mother realised that we wished to take a photograph and found a rough hairbrush and managed to get enough dust and dirt from her daughter's hair to bring it under some measure of control. It was a shame as she looked much cuter with it wild but it indicated the love and devotion that she felt. It was all Stig's mother could do but she did it well and with love. £7 a month would provide an education for Stig but how can you choose one child over the others – and how can you choose them all unless you are involved enough to ensure the money goes on education and not the father's drinking habit? But that is no excuse not to try.

Hinduism is arguably as much a cultural system as a religion that one is born into. The poor within Hinduism are judged to be poor because of 'bad karma' in a past life. This is inevitably counter to a spirit of generosity and philanthropy and is reflected in the vast gulf between rich and poor in India. Why should you give to the poor if god himself has ordained that you are born to be poor, and for your past sins should remain so? Fortunately not all Hindus

What hope for 'Stig' and these other children destined to a life in the brickworks.

share such a view but they remain in the minority. Booming India has not been reflected in booming generosity.

With such a vast number of people affected by caste prejudice it is surprising that there have not been mass uprisings and that the Dalits at least have not organized themselves into a movement. But this is to assume that they would not meet with violent opposition as it suits the purposes of the high caste to have the least popular jobs in society carried out by others and at very low cost. In addition, the uprisings in the Middle East at this time are assisted by the Internet and social networking which is largely unavailable to illiterates who are also of limited means. There has however been an increasing awareness around the world in recent years and growing voices internationally.

In 2001 Dr. Udit Raj, Chairman of the All India Confederation of Scheduled Castes led a campaign under the banner, 'Quit Hinduism,' and organized a mass rally in Delhi. However, despite having initially been granted permission for the event the police revoked the license at the last minute and 100's of thousands were turned away before they even reached the city. Undeterred the event was rescheduled and 10's of thousands gathered in their solidarity to end the caste system. It reveals a desire to make their voice heard and an indication of hope that the future may deliver change.

Ekta Parishad (Unity Forum) is an umbrella organisation that links hundreds of small campaigns across India, all fighting against economic and social injustices. Over the last 10 years, through a series of long marches in different states, it has built a strong movement with more than 200,000 members across 13 states.

Founded in 1991, Ekta has revitalised Mahatma Gandhi's message of non-violent action to deal with the problem of the widening gap between the rich and poor in India today. By organising marches and peaceful protests it brings marginalised groups together and supports India's rural communities' in their demands for justice, particularly control of rural livelihood resources; water, land and forests.

In October 2012, Ekta organised its second march 320 km from Gwalior to Delhi (Jansatyagraha 2012) to push the government to take action on land reforms. This time it had around 50,000 people on the road and by the time the march reached Agra, the Rural Development Minister, Jairam Ramesh was ready to sign a 10-point agreement meeting most of Ekta's demands. The march was then called off and people took trains back to all corners of India with copies of the agreement in their hands. This kind of people power may increasingly be a thorn in the side of the Indian Government as the poor gain a voice and demand justice.

The 2012 march of 50,000 Dalits demanding land rights
made the Government of India take note.

When I first visited India my work was centered in Uttar Pradesh, known as U.P, in the north of the country. It is a backward state with an estimated 45% literacy rate which is sometimes as low as 2% amongst Dalit women. In the town of Orai where we began our first school, you could live for years and never see another Western face. Many of U.P's villages have hardly changed at all in hundreds of years.

It was our practice, in those days, to travel to remote villages on push bike and on several occasions we were honored as the first white people to ever visit their community. It was always a humbling experience to be welcomed into the homes of village elders and to share our faith with such honorable people who, in the worlds eyes had nothing, but from whose lifestyle, community and stewardship the West has much to learn. We were freely welcomed and were free to share with these Hindu people but the same cannot be said of the darker face of the Hindutva militants.

When the Hindu BJP party came to power in 1998, in an attempt to promote Hinduism, they were quick to raise the false claim that people were being converted against their will and to begin the persecution of other religions. As well as locking the low caste and the Dalits into Hinduism it would perpetuate the caste system. In Orissa, attacks on Christians became violent and many were killed as houses were burned down and churches destroyed. Communities that had previously lived in harmony were subjected to mob rule and many were forced to flee for their lives. Thankfully things are calmer now but the laws introduced by the BJP party remain and proselytizing could result in imprisonment.

---

for further information on the caste system – we recommend reading Dalit Freedom by Joseph D'sousa – available from www.dfn.org.uk

CHAPTER 21

ROUGH JUSTICE

As I stated earlier – the judicial system in India was introduced by the British, but over the last century has become buried in bureaucracy and stained with corruption. Cases can take 10 to 20 years to be resolved and this, combined with the cost of going to trial means many cases never reach the courts and criminals escape with impunity.

Corruption is well documented within the police force and whilst not all police are corrupt, the pathetically low wages earned within the police force, inevitably leads to bribes being a substitute income to which a blind eye is turned by their superiors. That is to say a blind eye is turned as long as they receive their cut and this 'cut' is passed up the chain. Failing to do so will have serious consequences.

The national press, including respected journals such as The Hindu Times and The Times of India, are thorns in the side of politicians and are quick to expose and report corruption. Sadly, many of the cases that are revealed are because greedy fingers have failed to hand over their bosses cut of a bribe, and their zealous masters have then exposed their subordinates in an attempt to make themselves look righteous.

Bribes are endemic and woven within the culture of India and experienced by the lowly rickshaw driver seeking a license to the largest construction site under tender. Even applying for a passport will mean ones application may remain seated at the base of the processors in-tray until some extra rupees cross his palm.

I once traveled with my friend Paul Morley, to Calcutta by train and wished to purchase a ticket for the return journey. The main ticket office is a modern building with computerised systems where operators are seated behind glass partitions. A computerised print out on a notice board indicated that the train we wished to catch was full, and the next available seats were three days later. We were considering our options when a smart young man wearing a crisp and freshly pressed shirt and tie introduced himself and asked if we needed assistance. We explained our predicament and he informed us that, for 400 Rupees extra, around £5.50, there would be no problem in getting a ticket. We had no further business in Calcutta so reluctantly agreed to pay, but as we handed over the money a more senior and similarly smart gentleman arrived, to whom the young man bowed and then bent to touch the older man's feet. A short dialogue took place in Hindi and as the man left we enquired who he may be. 'Ah, he is my master, he taught me everything about my trade,' the young man replied with obvious sincerity. The trade to which he so passionately referred was that of ticket tout, as witnessed as the money now passed under the counter and into the till, following which a computerised ticket was produced and we were on our way.

We boarded the train later that day to find it was virtually empty. The whole thing was a scam. But not a scam aimed at the gullible tourist but at every user of this rail network. The Indians looked as bemused by the scheduled printout on the wall of the ticket office as we did. It is also inconceivable that this was going on without the station manager knowing about it and therefore the local government and no doubt passing all the way up to Delhi. Pay it upwards or face the consequences. 400 rupees was soon forgotten and worth it for the story, but as always it is the poor who suffer where such an amount may be punitive.

India is also well known for its harsh treatment of criminals and its prisoners and vigorous interrogation techniques are often used. These may include sleep deprivation, beatings, heads held under water in buckets, or even electric shock treatment. I have witnessed the vigour of the Indian police first hand when a camera was stolen from our car in Vijayawada some years ago. We had left the camera in the front foot well of the Ambassador we had hired whilst visiting an optician and under the supervisor of the driver. He had decided to stand guard outside the car but had failed to lock the door. He was temporarily distracted by someone asking for directions then out of the corner of his eye saw someone escaping down the street with the camera. He went in pursuit but lost him and returned in a very agitated fashion a few moments later to tell us what had happened. Paul Raju and the driver went to search again and amazingly returned about 10 minutes later, firmly holding the thief. He had been discovered sipping water in a coffee bar but the camera had vanished. On reflection, the thief was a good 20 pounds heavier than those who had apprehended him and it was surprising he hadn't put up more of a fight. He probably considered the same thing himself later that day whilst in police custody.

The police were called and the man arrested and taken into custody and we were required to give a statement later that day. We arrived at the police station and were taken into a small office where the thief was paraded in his underpants surrounded by several policemen. Whether it was because he anticipated a beating, had just received one or he was attempting to look contrite it was difficult to say, but he stood quivering slightly, and at this stage was pleading his innocence.

A sergeant sat at the desk, complete with pomaded moustache and wielding a stick which he used periodically and indiscriminately to strike the defendant with.

'The captain is coming,' he informed us, 'soon we will have a confession.'

In the corner of the room was a larger pole, about 5 ft long and 3 inches diameter and I was hoping that they were not going use this to beat a confession out of him.

After a short wait the Captain appeared in civilian uniform and carrying the demeanor of a bank manager rather than an interrogator. As I had feared, the large stick was to be put to good use but not as I had envisioned. The stick was placed behind the neck of the prisoner and the arms positioned on top in a form or crucifix position, then in a devilish contortion of woven rope, the construction was pulled tight.

'Soon we will have a confession.' The captain assured us. It was inevitable, as the muscles cramped into agonizing spasms, that only the most resolute of souls or hardiest of men would fail to confess, whether guilty or not. The confession soon followed and much to the delight of the captain, additional information followed that he was part of a gang originating from the southern state of Tamil Nadu that had been working in the area for some time. We were requested to return in the evening to meet the deputy chief of police. Vijayawada is a city of 2 million people and we were curious to know why such a senior figure would want to be involved it a relatively petty case.

At 9.00pm we were waiting in the police station when a cavalcade of several jeeps arrived containing the portly figure of the police chief. The Captain knew his position and after saluting quickly deferred his seat to his boss. It was explained to us that his officers were on their way to Tamil Nadu, 'as we speak,' to make various raids on property and that it was hoped that our goods would be recovered.

I was nervous that this case was attracting so much attention as we endeavor to keep a low profile to avoid any consequences for our staff, and it was unclear how much the face of the white man was responsible for this level of police resources. Sadly the 'Raj mentality' of many Indians is still to be swept aside. Amazingly, in a remarkable piece of detective work, the gang was arrested and a large amount of stolen goods were retrieved, including our camera.

The case went to court and two years later the camera, which had been held as evidence for the trial, was returned. The thief was released on bail but required to attend the court several times a month for the next five years at which time he would spend several months in jail or, if able, pay a fine.

There is little doubt that the man was guilty but one wonders how many innocent people are languishing in Indian jails because there accuser had more money to pay the judge and ensure the outcome was in their favour, or had simply given a forced confession under torture. And what prisons! For many years we had hoped to accompany Daniel Inbaraj, our school manager and pastor in Orai, who visited the local prison regularly to minister to the prisoners. When a new and more liberal Governor was employed a few years ago, we eventually were given permission and took a small team in to visit, and hold a meeting. The prisoners were kept 90 to a cell and released for only two hours a day. The men were not given pillows and only the thinnest of mats to sleep on. There was absolutely nothing to do from one monotonous day to the next. The temperature in Orai can reach 49 degrees in the summer and the heat can gather in one spot at an even higher temperature, then if the wind blows it in your direction, can cause a man to pass out. We were visiting in the relative mild of spring but what life was like in these cells in June does not bear consideration.

Paul Morley is a member of the magic circle of Christian Magicians and uses his skills as visual aids to communicate a story. It took a while to break the ice but when they realised that the heavily armed guards were laughing and enjoying the show, they too began to smile and laugh and for a moment at least, forget their hardship.

We spoke of God's love and promises for those who choose to believe in him, but it is hard to know how easily this was received by men who experienced such harsh punishment. Convicted murderers were mixed with fraudsters, rapists, petty thieves and those awaiting trial – yet to be convicted but unable to raise bail. We had brought oranges for the men and fans for their cells which the governor promised would be installed. As the prisoners queued to receive their small gift, one old man requested a Bible from us, which we freely gave, translated into his native language. Perhaps one man at least had recognised his guilt and received true forgiveness, even if not from the state of Uttar Pradesh.

In a remote village in Northern India we were garlanded by these gracious village people for being the first Westerners to ever visit. Paul Morley rewards them with a magic rope trick.

CHAPTER 22

WHERE TO NOW?

I mentioned the story earlier of the potter's daughter who wishes to be an air hostess and that she will be the first member of her family for generations to work away from home. In addition her potential income will allow her to be a part of 'shining' India's booming economy and at the same time a greater consumer, and inevitably – environmental polluter. I have sometimes wondered how the world will cope with the hundreds of millions of children seeking education in the developing world, who may then go on to contribute to the problems of global warming as they too move from a simple and sustainable lifestyle, to becoming modern consumers. Yet it is absolutely right that children in India should have the chance to escape poverty and the oppression that comes with their Dalit status. And who knows how many of them will have the scientific, political, environmental or social skills to make a massive change to society or the environment within this troubled yet amazing country.

India is predicted to overtake China and become the most populous nation in the world within 20 years. As India joins China, Russia, and Brazil in becoming the super powers of the future their continued growth will do little to ease the issues of climate change that are before us. Our children and grand children may well grow up in a very different world where, even in the developed nations, most people's disposable income will be spent, and wars may be fought over food and water rather than land and oil – a world that sees a booming population surviving on less available land, as it disappears beneath the sea through the melting polar ice cap, and the land that is left is devastated by unprecedented flood, drought and storms. I am just old enough to remember the day American President, John F. Kennedy was assassinated. At that time the population of the world was 3 billion. Sometime during 2011 a child was born that makes that figure 7 billion. By 2020 that figure could increase by a further .6 billion, similar to the entire population of the world in 1750.

Today more than 3.6 billion people are barely getting enough to eat with more than 1 billion of them in total abject poverty. India has more cases of malnutrition than the whole of sub Saharan Africa. And let us not forget that somewhere between 10 and 30 million children die every year of the worst possible death, starvation and starvation related diseases. If the wealthy nations do not face up to their obligations to the poor, then these figures will increase exponentially.

There are many other places in the world that need financial support and suffer the abuse of dictators, military conflict, famine and natural disasters. They all need help from the more wealthy nations as is their duty. But India is increasingly being ignored. It is after all a democracy and growing in financial strength at an unprecedented rate. But if one in three of the world's poor live there, it has the highest number of child laborers, and it is the world's center for people trafficking, it is a country that must be challenged. At the root of almost all India's human rights issues is the caste system and until the caste system is ended it will continue to make the lives of millions of people miserable.

Consider this. 500,000 people died in the tsunami that hit Indonesia on Boxing Day 2005 and we considered it a disaster on an unprecedented scale. 500,000 people have been made homeless in the Japanese earthquake and tsunami of 2011 and we were shocked at this human tragedy. Yet the Mumbai Government is in the advanced stages of their plans to demolish Dharavi and displace 500,000 people who will then be homeless and unable to earn a living. This is the same number that was affected by the disasters of Indonesia and Japan. Surely the world can no longer ignore the plight of the down trodden people that form the low caste and Dalit communities of India.

Apartheid came to an end through a movement of people of many nations with one voice and one message: – that apartheid is wrong. Through music people united around a song, 'Free Nelson Mandela' written by Jerry Dammers and people gathered in their tens of thousands at music festivals around the world. Perhaps it will take a similar movement of ordinary people to tackle this extraordinary phenomenon that has oppressed millions of people for millennia.

There is hope today for the Dalits. God's heart is for the poor and the marginalised, for the sick and the rejected, for those who suffer oppression and injustice, for the hungry and the homeless. And for all those who say 'why then doesn't He do something?' A voice comes back from heaven and says; 'why don't *you* do something?' – Everyone can do something.

The work of Life Association brings hope to children who would otherwise be hopeless, exploited and in many cases abused. And we are incredibly fortunate to have our candle products to raise awareness and finance for our work. 50% of the sale of each of our clay cup candles purchased online goes directly towards our work in India and also covers our overheads. We are therefore uniquely privileged so that every penny of our child sponsorship programme goes directly to the children, without additional administration costs. To sponsor a child with Life Association costs just £20 a month and provides a loving home, as well as healthcare, education, food and clothing. If you are a tax payer, then this amount gift aided adds another 25p in every pound to our work.

£20.00 a month provides hope and meets all the needs of boys like Nani and Rajender who live and study at one of our children's homes. They were rag pickers spending their days in the blazing heat on the rubbish tip collecting scraps from amongst broken glass, animal entrails and household waste for just .50p a day – or Sunny who was the son of a prostitute. His mother died of Aids when he was just six when we found him on the streets in the Red Light District with no one to care for him.

Our children's programme in Mumbai, where Sunny now lives, provides a home for 10 boys or 10 girls who come from some of the most difficult backgrounds from the streets of Mumbai or are rescued from child prostitution. They are adopted for life into a loving Christian home. To fund one of these children's homes costs just £200 a month and provides all the needs of the children and the adoptive parents who care for them.

The Dalits have suffered extreme levels of discrimination, persecution and abuse for over 3000 years but there is hope. Never before has it been possible to communicate and mobilise people through the Internet and social networking as it is today. As people become aware of these issues they can act by joining us and other likeminded organisations to raise awareness and apply pressure on international governments to cause India to enforce their existing laws, and end the caste system forever.

We still plan to build 50 schools and children's homes through our charity. That will be a good thing but it is not enough. We know that the real issue behind the poverty that afflicts millions in India is the caste system. We will not bring about a significant change to a substantial number of people without this issue being addressed.

I hope that my story challenges people to give by supporting a child. This makes a massive difference to their lives and is a sign of a longer term commitment which is what it takes to make real change. I hope that business men who read this will not wait as long as I did or have to lose everything before finding their Kingdom purpose. The question that must be asked by the rich is; 'How much is enough.' I believe that true happiness, purpose and godliness can be found in squaring this question, which is only ever between you and God anyway, and nothing to do with anyone else, then being liberated to give away what is left. I have spent many years looking at the thousands of scriptures that relate to finance and am well on the way to recording them in a book. I even know the title. – It is called the King's New Clothes and I hope that soon after you read this it may be available and the intriguing title explained. If you are not yet convinced, I hope at that time you may be persuaded that working on Kingdom business is also right for you.

If you would like to know more about the work of Life Association you can visit our web site at www.lifeassociation.co.uk or visit our online store at www.dalit.co.uk or e-mail us at info@lifeassociation.co.uk.

Even better, if you want to help us meet the needs of some of the most desperate children on the planet today, would you consider completing the next page of this book and posting it to Life Association, Sitch House, Taxal, Whaley Bridge, High Peak, SK23 7EA. England, or you can download a version at our Life Association web site or donate by credit card online or by phoning our office on 01663 734374. Or why not visit one of our projects. If this book has challenged you then that is nothing compared to the challenge of seeing this work first hand. We run several trips a year in partnership with Soapbox and would love to have you along. For more information about these trips contact projects@soapboxtrust.com

Be warned – it may just change your life as well.

ABOUT THE AUTHOR

Simon Hawthorne is a serial entrepreneur. During his 30 years in the fashion business he has also set up a music, retail and wholesale business; had nine retail fashion shops, a 24-hour multi-head embroidery business; imported stone flags from India; launched a Fairtrade and organic street fashion clothing brand named Ascension; and held licenses for Umbro, Ben Sherman, Lonsdale and The Football Association. During this time he co-launched The Message Trust, with his brother Andy.

During the 1980's he played lead guitar in the Bill Mason Band, a pioneering Christian punk/new wave band that were known for their uncompromising proclamation of their faith and recorded their one and only album – No Sham.

For 18 of his 30 years in business he has also worked in India, building schools and orphanages, before going full time with his charity Life Association and launching Dalit Candles, manufactured in the Dharavi slum in Mumbai to help raise awareness of the plight of the Dalits and funds for his charity.

He lives on a farm in the Peak District with his wife Julia and where they indulge their love of animals. Julia also works full time with the charity. They have two sons, Adam and Daniel.

ABOUT THE CHARITY

For 18 years Life Association has been working amongst the Dalit people of India, building schools, orphanages and children's homes in some of the poorest parts of the country. All of their work is in association with a local evangelical Christian church.

In addition to the practical work on the ground they also work to raise awareness of the plight of the Dalits and the difficult issues they face.

In 2010 the charity launched its brand – Dalit Candles that are made in the Dharavi slum in Mumbai, India's largest slum, to raise funds for the charity and awareness for the Dalits. These are now available on line and in gift shops, florists, delicatessens and Christian book shops throughout the UK.

Life Association staff are available to speak at events where their multi-media presentations bring to life the real issues of the caste system.

stewardship®

Stewardship's fund for: Life Association Ltd

Your personal details

Surname _____ Title _____

Forenames _____

Address _____

_____ Postcode _____

Daytime Tel _____

Email _____

Stewardship will communicate with you by email unless otherwise specified here. Please use post ☐

Do you already have an account with us?   ☐ No   ☐ Yes, Account No: _____

For a regular gift

Amount: £ _____ Start date: ___/___/_____ (please allow 3 weeks)

Frequency: ☐ Monthly   ☐ Quarterly   ☐ Six-Monthly   ☐ Annually   (minimum £10)

For a one-off gift

I enclose a cheque payable to Stewardship for £ _____ (min.£30) (please staple cheque to this form)

This gift should be regarded as

☐ An anonymous gift

☐ A non Gift Aided gift (In this case, please do not sign the Gift Aid declaration)

Gift Aid Declaration (to authorise tax reclaims on gifts to Stewardship)

I declare my intention that tax should be recovered under the Gift Aid Scheme on all donations I make to Stewardship (both in future and for the past four years) until further notice. I understand that I must pay enough income tax or capital gains tax for each tax year that is at least equal to the amount of tax that Stewardship will reclaim on my giving.

Signature _____ Date _____

Ref: 20010161

By completing and returning this form, you acknowledge that you have read and understood the points listed under 'Things you need to know' overleaf.

Direct Debit Instruction

Name & address of your Bank/Building Soc

To _____ Bank/Building Soc

_____

_____

Postcode _____

Name(s) of Account Holder(s)

[_____]

Bank/Building Society account Number

☐☐☐☐☐☐☐☐ Banks and Building Societies may not accept Direct Debit instructions for some types of account

Branch Sort Code

☐☐ ☐☐ ☐☐

Date: _____

Service User Number

| 9 | 8 | 2 | 1 | 1 | 7 |

Ref Number - office use only

☐☐☐☐☐☐☐☐

DIRECT Debit

Stewardship,
Freepost (EDO 5086),
Loughton, Essex IG10 3BR

Instruction to your Bank/Building Society
Please pay Stewardship Direct Debits from the account detailed on this instruction subject to the safeguards assured by the Direct Debit guarantee. I understand this instruction may remain with Stewardship and, if so, details will be passed electronically to my Bank/Building Society.

Signature(s): _____

Print Name(s): _____

SEND TO STEWARDSHIP, NOT YOUR BANK/BUILDING SOCIETY

Supporting **Life Association Ltd**

We're really pleased that you've decided to join us in supporting Life Association Ltd.

You can give in this way thanks to our giving service, which means that we will reclaim tax worth 25% under Gift Aid. The work of Life Association Ltd has been approved by Stewardship as charitable and is therefore eligible to receive grants from us.

4 simple steps

Getting started in supporting Life Association Ltd with Stewardship couldn't be easier.

1. Complete the application form and Direct Debit instruction. N.B: If you would prefer to keep your identity anonymous please tick the box on the form.
2. Make a note of your giving and detach this page (which includes your Direct Debit Guarantee overleaf) and keep it somewhere safe.
3. If you wish to send a cheque, please make it payable to Stewardship and attach it to the form.
4. Return your form direct to us: Stewardship, Freepost (EDO 5086), Loughton Essex IG10 3BR

what happens next?

Upon receiving your form we will set things in motion to fulfil your giving request. You will hear back from us to confirm that everything is in order with your gift to us. We will pass on a confirmation to Life Association Ltd to let them know of your wish to help support them, unless of course you've chosen to remain anonymous.

changing your support in future

If you wish to change your regular giving in future, or make additional one-off gifts in support of this, or other eligible recipients, please contact a member of our giving services team on **020 8502 8560** or giving@stewardship.org.uk.

my record of giving

Use this section to keep a record of your support for Life Association Ltd

Amount: £ _____

Start date: ___/___/_____

One-off? ☐

Frequency: ☐ Monthly ☐ Quarterly
☐ Six-monthly ☐ Annually

Anonymous? ☐

organise more of your giving

By using Stewardship's giving service to support Life Association Ltd you will automatically have a full giving account available to use should you wish. You can use this account to organise all of your giving under one roof with just one Direct Debit. For more details visit **www.stewardship.org.uk/give**.

I would like to support the work of Life Association in the following way -

☐ I would like to sponsor a child at a cost of £20.00 a month.
☐ I would like to sponsor a home for street children at £200.00 a month
☐ I would like to make a one off gift of £_____
☐ I would let to set up a regular standing order of £_____
☐ Please debit my card £_____

Card Number _____
Expiry Date --/-- Security code _____ (last 3 digits on signature strip)
(For Switch: issue number ___Start date: __/__
☐ Please add me to your database.

My Details:

Title & Full name: _____
Address: _____
_____
_____Postcode:_____
Telephone_____Mobile_____
Email:_____

Gift Aid -
I am a UK tax payer and would like Life Association to reclaim tax on all my donations as from the 1st April 2011.

Signed: _____Date:_____

*I pay income tax and /or capital gains tax at least equal to the tax that Life Association will reclaim from my donations (currently 25p for each £1 you give). Please notify Life Association if your name, address or status changes.

If you're donation is gift aided please return this page to -
Stewardship, Freepost (EDO 5086), Loughton, Essex IG10 3BR

For all other donations please return this page to -
Sitch House, Taxal, Whaley Bridge, High Peak, SK23 7EA.

Reg. Charity #1115262